MW01145135

He's Waiting . . .
At The Well

Crystal Duncan-Hogue

Unless otherwise indicated, all scriptural quotations are from the *King James Version* of the Bible.

HE'S WAITING AT THE WELL
Crystal Duncan-Hogue

To contact the author or obtained additional copies of this book, please visit our website:
www.crystalhogueministries.org
email: info@crystalhogueministries.org

ISBN # 978-0-9791939-6-5

Published, Designed, and printed by:
Heavenly Printing
Chicago, Illinois • 773-783-2981
service@heavenlyprinting.com

Table of Contents

Special Acknowledgements

I would first like to thank my God and Savior, the Lord Jesus Christ. I love you so much. You are an awesome God! Thank you for the gifts you have given me. I give my gifts back to you using them to win souls to Jesus Christ around the world.

To my dear sister, Sherry: You have always believed in me and encouraged me to write. Because of your advice, I stuck with it. I love you and thank you for believing in me.

I would also like to thank my mother and friend, Dr. Carolyn Duncan, who never stopped praying for me. You have always been there. As a first lady, God has given you the strength to endure and survive the attacks of the enemy. Thank you for your faithful prayers, your words of wisdom, and ministry. I love you.

To my father and Pastor, Bishop Duncan, thank you, Daddy, for raising me in the church. Thank you for your tender guidance, your strength and your words of wisdom. The Bible says to *train up a child the way that he should go and when he is older it will not depart from it.* God's Word has never departed from me because I have hidden it in my heart. Thanks for always being there Daddy; I love you.

To my five brothers: RH Jr., who is like my second father, I could always count on you when I needed advice. You have such an anointing of wisdom on your life. Thanks for being there for me big brother. I love you. To Ivan, the brother who scared the boys away (smile): I love you. To Derrick, or should I say my twin (almost): You are definitely one of a kind. Your charisma and your good looks are too much for the women. I love you. To Adrian, my partner in music: I love you. Thanks for taking time to produce my gospel CD, "Stand Still." The way you put music and sounds together is incredible. You have a unique style and gift that was given to you by God. Use it for His glory! To my younger brother Isaac, who is like my own son: I remember changing your diapers and look at you now, handsome and all grown up. You are the silent one, even though your names means laughter, but I love you. Thank you all for believing in me.

To all of my close friends, relatives and spiritual leaders, thanks for praying me through and being there. Thanks to my past and present pastors, Bishop and Sis. Brazier in Chicago; Bishop and Evangelist Gwin in Champaign; and Bishop and Dr. Duncan in Indianapolis. Thank you for your great leadership and giving me the opportunities to use my gifts within various ministries.

To my family, my three children, Kahlil, Clarissa and Andrew: Kahlil, your brilliance will take you far in life. I am so proud of you. You are my joy. Your smile brightens my day! I thank God for you and I love you. Clarissa, I've watched you develop into a beautiful young lady. Put God first in everything that you do and you will go far. Watch out for the boys and stay on the right path. I love you! Drew (the drummer), God has blessed you with an amazing talent. Use it for His glory. You are so talented and good looking, but watch out for the girls and stay on the right path so God may bless you. I love you.

And finally, to my dear husband, Charles Hogue: Baby, you hold a special place in my heart and I will always love you. Thank you for your enduring love and support.

May God shower all of you with his blessings! I love you all.

The Samaritan Woman

John 4:5-26

Then cometh he (Jesus) to a city of Samaria which is called Sychar, near the plot of ground that Jacob gave to his son Joseph. Now Jacob's well was there. Jesus therefore, being wearied with his journey, sat thus on the well, and it was about the sixth hour. There cometh a woman of Samaria to draw water. Jesus saith unto her, give me a drink. For his disciples were gone away unto the city to buy meat. Then saith the woman of Samaria unto him, how is it that thou being a Jew ask a drink of me, which am a woman of Samaria, for the Jews have no dealings with the Samaritans. Jesus answered and said unto her, if thou knewest the gift of God, and who it is that saith to thee, give me to drink, thou wouldest have asked of him, and he would have given thee living water. The woman saith unto him, sir, thou has nothing to draw with, and the well is deep, from whence then hast thou that living water? Are you greater than our father Jacob, which gave us the well, and drank thereof himself and his children, and his cattle? Jesus answered and said unto her, whosoever drinketh of this water shall thirst again, but whosoever drinketh of the water that I shall give him shall never thirst, but the water that I shall give him shall be in him a well of water springing up into everlasting life. The woman saith unto him, sir give me this water, that I thirst not, neither come here to draw. Jesus said to her, go call your husband and come here. The woman said, "I have no husband." Jesus said to her, "you have well said, I have no husband, for you have had five husbands and the one whom you now have is not your husband, in that you spoke truly." The woman said to Him, "Sir, I perceive that you are a prophet. Our fathers worshiped on this mountain, and you Jews say that in Jerusalem is the place where one ought to worship. Jesus said to her, woman, believe me, the hour is coming when you will neither on this mountain, nor in Jerusalem, worship the father. You worship what you do not know, we know what we worship, for salvation is of the Jews. But the hour is coming, and now is, when the true worshipers will worship the Father in spirit and truth for the father is seeking such to worship Him. God is Spirit, and those who worship Him must worship Him in spirit and in truth. The woman said to Him," I know that Messiah is coming (who is called Christ). When He comes, He will tell us all things." Jesus said to her, I who speak to you am He." The woman dropped her water bucket beside the well and went back to the village and told everyone.

Jesus had left Capernaum, a city where the Samaritans lived, to go to Jerusalem for the Passover. This journey took three days. The Jews often avoided Samaria by going around it along the Jordan River. The hatred between the Jews and Samaritans went back to the days of the Exile. The Jews hated the Samaritans and considered them to be no longer pure Jews. However, Jesus needed to go through Samaria. Note: He *needed* to go through Samaria because of a need that Je had to fulfill. He knew a woman needed him. He heard a soul crying out desperately to Him in the desert. He knew that a broken woman with a broken heart needed a drink of his living water . . . a Samaritan Woman.

I am giving this Samaritan woman a name and a story. We really don't know what her story is except the fact that she was married five times and she was living with a man that wasn't her husband. I will call her . . . Taliah. She had gone from one man to another, going from one bad relationship to the next. However, we can't be too quick to judge her, because during biblical times a husband could write a certificate of divorce for several reasons. Deuteronomy 24:1-4 states, *When a man takes a wife and marries her, and it happens that she finds no favor in his eyes because he has found some uncleanness in her, then let him write her a certificate of divorce, put it in her hand, and send her out of his house. When she has departed from his house, and goes and becomes another man's wife, if the latter husband detests her and writes her a certificate of divorce, puts it in her hand, and sends her out of his house, or if the latter husband dies who took her as his wife, then her former husband who divorced her must not take her back to be his wife after she has been defiled.* Confusing isn't it. So all five husbands divorced her, and it was accepted, according to the book of the law.

We don't really know the real reason why she ended up with five husbands. All we know is that they all divorced her. It's obvious that they no longer desired, wanted, or needed her. Whatever the reason, they left her alone . . . by herself, only to meet another . . . who would yet break her heart . . . again. Just when she thought she'd discovered the perfect love, her heart was torn to pieces again. She went to another to try to put the pieces back together, only to realize that he couldn't because of all the baggage left from the previous relationship. Then she discovers he too didn't want her. Tossed from man to man, she continues to search for love in all the wrong faces to make her whole and complete. She doesn't realize that they could never make her whole and complete, and that she should never depend on a man for her happiness.

She continued to search for men to fill the void that was so deep inside her soul. She desperately wanted to be loved and needed by a man. Have you been there? She needed to know what true love was. Don't you? She was thirsty for love from a man. I think all of us women long for a man to really love us. Yes, even you; and don't act like you don't. It doesn't matter what age you are, sixteen or seventy-five, never been married, want to get married, divorced, widowed, or living with a man (and you shouldn't be). God created you for the man. As a matter of fact, He took you out of the man, so you are the other half of a man. Therefore, we desire to have a man because we are already part of a man. Get it? We need to be held by one, to be loved by one, and be cherished by one. We yearn to have a close relationship with a man; a oneness. Genesis 3:16 reads, *your desire shall be towards your husband.* However, some of you, yes even you, desire more than one, and you know that's not right. One is enough. You are like Taliah searching for love in all the wrong faces.

In Taliah's case, the search was for men; many of them and plenty of them. All different types: tall, short, good-looking, ugly, rich, poor, white, black - it really didn't matter as long as he was a man. Not one or two, but six. Yes six! Please don't start judging her. Don't act like you haven't had your share of men too. As a matter of fact, how many men have you had? Think about it. Think back to all the men in your life, since high school, that have either hurt you, rejected you, mistreated you, used you up, abused you, raped you, disrespected you, left you with a baby, or babies, etc. So don't act like you are Miss or Mrs. "holier than thou." I'm sure you probably had your share of men too.

I have to admit, I've had my share of men too. When I was younger and didn't have my head on straight, in a backslidden state, running from my calling, like Jonah. I too was searching for love in all the wrong places and in all the wrong faces. But thank God I was healed, delivered and set free when I met Him at the well. "Him who?" Glad you ask. Jesus Christ; the one who changed my life forever; the one who caused me to drop my water bucket . . . at the well. By the way, have you dropped your water bucket? Once I tasted of His love and drank of His Spirit (the Living Water) and ate the food (His Word) which He so eagerly prepared for me and invited me to share with Him at His dinner table. He said, *"Come and dine* with me and *come and sup with me,* I came because He began to draw me. So I drank and drank of the living water that He so freely offered to me at the well, as a gift, and it was oh so sweet and so good! *Oh taste and see that the Lord is good, blessed is the man* or woman *that trusts in Him.* A real woman trusts Him with her life, her finances, her marriage, her job, her future plans . . . her everything. I have tasted and seen that He is really good so I can't help but to trust Him. Once you have tasted of the gift, how could you go back? How could you pick up your water bucket again? How could you go back to your old ways? *If any man be in Christ he is a new creature, old things are passed away all things are become new.* How could you put those men before God? Those men whom you have made idols? Yes idols - choosing them before God. God said *I am a jealous God I will have no gods before me.* Again, how could you have once tasted of the gift and then return back? It's like *a dog returning to his own vomit.*

I took a drink and it was exactly what I needed. It caused me to drop my water bucket. Once I realized that I no longer needed the water that I thought I needed to quench my thirst, I drank.

I drank and then I drank some more of His living water. I couldn't get enough! His Holy Spirit filled me up so much that I am overflowing with His love. So much so that;
~ He causes me to dance
~ He causes me to sing
~ He causes me to laugh
~ He causes me to worship Him in spirit and in truth
~ He causes me to praise Him with all of me
~ He causes me to weep tears of joy uncontrollably
~ He causes me to want more of Him
    Every day
    Early in the morning
    Yearning
    To hear his voice
    To feel His touch

His presence
Once again
To breathe on me.

Jesus, please breathe on me again and again! *Cast me not away from thy presence and please don't ever take your Holy Spirit from me!* He causes me to do whatever is necessary to please Him, to serve Him, to never want to disappoint Him. He moves me to humble myself and be the servant that He has called me to be. He causes me to live my life for Him, and Him alone. Jesus has changed me so that I can't find enough words to describe it. It goes beyond what the human mind can even comprehend. And that's why I just have to tell somebody, anybody, everybody, about Him! Ladies and Gentleman, I present to you . . . Jesus. Yes, that's right, give Him your best applause, because He deserves it. He is real and He is exactly what you have been searching for all your life. You need Him. He is not some fairy tale out of a storybook. He is the real Prince Charming. He is the book, or should I say, the Word made flesh and He dwells among us.

Christianity is not about religion, coming to church every Sunday, or Wednesday Bible Study or being involved in several ministries. It's about having a relationship with Jesus Christ. His love is so deep and its real- not counterfeit. And no man . . . no dog . . . no career . . . no friends . . . no family . . . no lover . . . no fame or fortune can ever take away the love that I have for Him. I love Him because He first loved me and nothing can ever separate me from His love. *Who shall separate us from the love of Christ? Shall tribulations or distress, persecutions, famine, or nakedness, or peril, or sword?*

As it is written, for thy sake we are killed all the day long, we are accounted as sheep for the slaughter. Nay in all these things we are more than conquerors through Him that loved us. For I am persuaded, that neither death, nor life, nor angels, nor principalities, nor powers, nor things present, nor things to come, nor height, nor depth, nor any other creature, shall be able to separate us from the love of God, which is in Christ Jesus our Lord. Wow! What a Love!

However, Taliah didn't know about this love. So she began to search for love in all the wrong faces. She searched for love in men. She needed them desperately to fulfill her, validate her, to love her, to need her, to desire her, and to want her. She was so desperate and thirsty for love from them. What she failed to realize is that she could never find true unconditional love in a man because God is love. Men could never quench the thirst in the depths of her soul. That's why they kept breaking her heart. After all the times her heart was broken, she soon began to realize something was missing.

Well it's about time Taliah! It really wasn't men that she needed. Or was it? Well, as her journey unfolds, I will tell you her story. Taliah has her bucket swinging in her hand and is on her way now to draw water from the well. She is walking in a long, hot desert. She is thirsty and by herself, with a lot of thoughts racing through her mind about her past and current relationships with men. She has so many questions. She has entered a season of wilderness in her life and is searching for answers. While she gets lost on her journey, she encounters a few things. She meets an unexpected man, a Jew, who is waiting and watching . . . simply waiting and watching her while she tries everything and everybody else - especially men - before coming to Him. She doesn't realize that Jesus is whom she really needs. And so, her journey begins to the well.

Chapter One

Seasons

Ecclesiastes 3:1
   "To every thing there is a season, and a time to every purpose under the heaven . . ."

There are various seasons in life. In the natural, we have the fall, spring, summer and winter seasons. In the fall you enjoy the beauty of the colorful leaves on the trees and watch them fall softly through the wind. In the spring you plant bulbs and watch them bloom into beautiful flowers, pink, red and yellow roses and white and purple lilies. The sky is softly blue with white clouds forming. The grass is beautifully green. You feel the cool breeze from the spring wind while you watch beautiful yellow butterflies dance in the wind. The smell of morning raindrops is refreshing when you take a walk through the park.

   In the summer, there's hot weather, family vacations, beaches, cruises. At night you can feel the summer breeze as you open your patio door. The cricket sounds outside your bedroom window at night relaxes you to sleep. But then the winter comes: cold, bitter, windy storms and icy and snowy blizzards. The winter season seems so very long. Sometimes, even cities that are not equipped to handle the winter shut down because of so much snow when there's a bad winter storm. The winter season seems to go on and on. It's in some comparison to the wilderness . . . never ending and to some, it is depressing. When you enter the season of wilderness in your life, it is a difficult and trying time. Sometimes you find yourself alone, depressed and isolated. However, it is in those times when the Lord reveals himself to you. His Spirit comforts you and reminds you that He is there. His still small voice says: *I will never leave you nor forsake you; I am with you even unto the end of the age. I will not put more on you then what you are able to bear.* God is there with you every step of the way. When you think, within your flesh, you just can't make it through this journey, this season of wilderness, in your spirit the Holy Spirit whispers softly, *you can do all things through Jesus Christ who strengthens you.*

It's amazing how one can find the beauty in an unpleasant situation, whatever situation it may be. But let's compare it to the winter season. The winter may appear depressing from the natural when you see that the clouds are dreary and grey and it's bitter cold. However, when you look at it from a spiritual point of view, you start noticing the white in the snow and how beautiful it lays on the trees. You notice the warmth from the fire in the fireplace, the sound of the whistling wind in the winter storm, the beauty of the Christmas season, the smell of the pine in the trees, and the most important event of all is the celebration of the birth of our Lord and Savior Jesus Christ. And yes, it did happen. Jesus Christ was born! Even though He is God, He was yet manifested into flesh.

Wow! God loved the world so much that He became flesh - one hundred percent God, yet one hundred percent flesh. How can that be? I'm glad you asked. *But without controversy, great is the mystery of God. For God was manifested into flesh, justified in the spirit, seen by angels, preached to the gentiles, believed on the world and ascended up to glory.* I can just stay right there talking about how awesome the mystery of the Godhead is. But let's get back to the winter season and then back to Taliah. Stay with me, I'm going somewhere.

Just like you can find the beauty in the winter season,

you can also find the beauty in your wilderness experience, tests, trials, sickness, valley experience and whatever else breaks your spirit. Solomon says, in Proverbs 17:22, *a merry heart does good like a medicine, but a broken spirit dries the bones.* Having a broken spirit is not good for your body. However, no matter what the problem is, or what has caused your spirit to be broken, you can still yet rejoice. The apostle Paul said, *Most gladly therefore will I rather glory or (rejoice) in my infirmities, so that the power of Christ may rest upon me!* Isn't that awesome? Who cares about the troubles of this world when you have the power of Christ resting upon you right in the midst of the trouble?

When there is a thunderstorm coming, have you ever noticed how the clouds gather together very low, and it becomes dark outside? The wind gets still, lightning strikes first lighting up the sky, but there's no sound yet. Then the thunder comes, and finally the rain. But I have never known a storm to last that long, have you? Immediately after the storm, a rainbow appears *(covenant, a promise made by God),* the sun shines and you notice the storm has passed over. Praise God! Hallelujah! The storm has passed over. Next time you experience a storm in your life, remember to rest in the storm and look for the rainbow; the storm will not last very long. Rest and have peace knowing that God is in control.

Jesus was resting in the boat during a terrible storm, while his disciples were panicking saying, *"Master, Master we are perishing?"* In other words or to paraphrase, "Why are you sleeping at a time like this? Don't you care that we are perishing?" They didn't realize who was in the storm with them. Or, for that matter, who created the storm. Peter, John, and James chill out - the master is on board. Don't worry, rest; for I will calm the storm. Now, if Jesus can rest in the storm, how about you? It's easy to rest in your storm knowing that Jesus is right there with you, isn't it?

Like natural seasons, there are also various spiritual

seasons that you must go through as a child of God. You must go through a season of preparation, a season of growth, a season of perfecting your character, a season of silence, and a season of doors being shut, a season of harvest, a season of blessings, a season of suffering, and a season when your destiny is finally birthed. Solomon talks about it in the book of wisdom. *To everything there is a season, and a time or purpose under the heaven* . . . So wait, your timing is not God's timing. Trust that God is working behind the scenes on your behalf, even during your winter season.

Taliah doesn't realize that she has entered her winter season until after she is out of her wilderness. She couldn't see or spiritually discern because she was blinded by her pain, and had no connection with the Master. Her journey begins in the hot desert, through her wilderness season, going to the well to get a drink of water that will quench her thirst, or so she thinks. But there was someone unexpected at the well. There is a man, a Jew, who is waiting and watching her, wanting to offer her a drink of living water that only He could give her. This was an offer that she later realized that she could not refuse. Refuse this water that was given to her by the long awaited Messiah . . . in person . . . at the well . . . in the desert . . . talking to her so sweetly . . . so gently and kindly with concern in his voice about her, a broken Samaritan Woman?

No. I don't think so. Refusing this water is not an option because this is the only thing that can satisfy her. Could it be Him? Yes, Taliah, it is He. For she heard His voice, a powerful voice that said, *"I who is speaking to you . . . am He."* It sounded like *a voice in the thunder* . . . or *in the wind* . . . or *in the waters;* but more like *a still small voice* softly whispering in the depths of her broken heart. Taliah meets the Messiah, Jesus Christ, at the well and drank of the living water that quenched her thirst and changed her life forever. There . . . at the well . . . in the hot desert . . . with her dropped bucket . . . she discovers truth, and *the truth made her free.*

Chapter Two

A Journey
In The Wilderness

Hosea 2:14
   "Therefore, I will allure her into the desert and speak comfortably to her."

Taliah walked alone silently in the desert. While she was walking, she imagined that she was walking along an oceans' shore, listening to the sounds of the blue waves rushing against the white sands. The red sunset is resting behind the mountains leaving its' shadow across the ocean's breast. The white seagulls soared high above the sky trying to catch the wind. She can feel the warmth of the sunrays against the back of her neck. As she walks, her mind is twisted and screaming with thoughts racing back and forth giving her a migraine headache.

   Ouch, that hurts! She has so much pain and aching inside; not just in her head, but in her soul. She asks herself, "When will the pain, confusion, guilt, depression, and loneliness cease?" Her emotions are swimming around in her soul trying to find a resting place. "When will my emotions stop riding this roller coaster and when will this ride stop. Better yet, when can I get off of it?" She had so many questions and no one to answer them. She has concluded that she has entered into a different season of her life, and she is not quite sure what this season is called. Perhaps it is a season called the wilderness. Therefore, she is unable to enjoy the beauty of nature like the rushing sounds of the white waves across the ocean, the singing of the blue birds, the captivating view of the red sunset, the serenity of the deep teal ocean and the gentle breeze brushing against her skin blowing swiftly through the strands of her long curly hair.

Reality brings her mind back. There is no ocean to view, there are no blue birds singing, she can't even feel a cool breeze from the wind. She feels nothing but hot air, making it almost impossible for her to breathe. "I am so thirsty," she thought. "I can't wait to get a drink from the well." As she was thinking on these things, she stumbled across a bush of red roses, smack dab in the middle of the desert. "Now how can roses survive in this hot desert, with no water?" She stopped and studied the roses for a minute and wondered how something so beautiful and delicate could have thorns and be in this desert. She picked one of the roses off the bush to put in her hair and a thorn from the bush poked her finger. "Oh you dumb rose bush!" she said. She wiped the blood on her skirt and continued walking.

"Oh if I could breathe fresh air again!" she thought. If only I could exhale and breathe into my life true happiness. If only I could find the answers. But how? My heart feels so broken . . . shattered . . . dirty and wicked. And it needs severe mending . . . repairing . . . healing . . . cleaning . . . and, come to think of it, I need a whole new heart." Her spirit has been broken and she has lost the will and the strength to even go on. Taliah is singing the woe is me song and creating a pity party right in the desert. However, what she doesn't realize is only the Master, the Savior, the one who died for her, her Redeemer, Savior, whose name is Jesus, is the only one who can heal her broken heart and make her whole again. She doesn't realize that she can cry out, *Lord, create within me a clean heart and renew the right spirit within me*, like the psalmist David said! She doesn't realize that Jesus has been sitting at the well, patiently waiting for her and watching her while she searched for love in all the wrong places and in all the wrong faces. He's been watching her while she tries everything and everybody else, trying everything possible to quench the thirst within her soul that she so desperately needs filled. While she was depressed, lost in her pain and in the depths of her hidden tears, a powerful, yet gentle, still small voice speaks comfortably and tenderly to her, speaking life into her. *Therefore, I will allure her into the desert and speak comfortably to her.* Yet she can't hear the voice because her mind is bombarded with negative thoughts, painful memories of bad relationships, and nothing good.

I will come back to Taliah in a moment, but this is a good place to take a note. Nowadays, people are thirsty. They are thirsty for so many different things to fill that void that only God can fill. People have tried to fill that void with money, sex, drugs, alcohol, relationships, families, careers, ministries, fame, and the list goes on. They do not realize that the only one that can fill that void is Jesus Christ.

Chapter Three

Money Is The Root Of All Evil

I Timothy 6:10
"For the love of money is the root of all evil: which while some coveted after, they have erred from the faith, and pierced themselves through with many sorrows."

People are hungry for money, not realizing that money is the root of all evil. Yes, we need money to survive, but don't we always want more? Sometimes when people look at celebrities with their black BMW and Mercedes Benz, their mansion on the hill, and their fine clothes and jewelry, they think they would be fine if they could just have what they have. Be careful; that's covetousness. Luke 12:15 reads: *Take heed and beware of covetousness, for one's life does not consist in the abundance of the things he possesses.* So beware of wanting to be like someone else because of the things they have. Life is not about things.

This world is only temporary. Don't think a large bank account will solve all your problems. Don't get me wrong. It's good to have a cushion in your bank account to be comfortable. You need money to survive. The problem comes when that money becomes an idol and you forget God. *If you seek ye first the kingdom of God (give him his 10% and more) then all of these things shall be added unto you.* Some of the richest and most famous people are also some of the unhappiest people. They are lonely, miserable and hiding behind their large bank accounts. They throw large parties. If they want something, they get it.

It doesn't matter if it's clothing, furniture, cars, property, drugs, alcohol and even people. Sometimes they even buy people (prostitutes) to spend time with them and to satisfy their fleshly desires.

Solomon states *enjoying the pleasures of life is all vanity.* I think it's important to share this with you because money can hinder people from finding Jesus at the well. In Ecclesiastes Chapter 2, Solomon quotes, *I said in my heart come now, I will test you with mirth (fun), therefore enjoy pleasure, (gratify the flesh) but surely, this was vanity (pride). I said of laughter, madness and of mirth, what does it accomplish? I searched in my heart how to gratify my flesh with wine, (drink and be merry) while guiding my heart with wisdom, and how to lay hold on folly (foolish acting, jestoring) so I might see what was good for sons (or daughters) to do under heaven all the days of their lives. I made my works great; I built myself houses, and planted myself vineyards. I made myself gardens and orchards, and I planted all kinds of fruit trees in them.*

I made myself water pools from which to water the growing trees of the grove. I acquired male and female servants, and had servants born in my house. (Solomon thought he had it going on, didn't he?) I had greater possessions of herds and flock than all were in Jerusalem before me. I also gathered for myself silver and gold (expensive jewelry) and the special treasures of kings and of the provinces. I acquired male and female singers (entertainment) the delights of the sons of men, and musical instruments of all kinds. So I became great and excelled more than all who were before me in Jerusalem. Also my wisdom remained with me. Whatever my eyes desired I did not keep from them. I did not withhold my heart from any pleasure. My heart rejoiced in all my labor. And this was my reward from all my labor. Then I looked on all the works that my hands made, and on the labor in which I had toiled, and indeed all was vanity and grasping for the wind. There was no profit under the sun.

So in other words, all that Solomon had was vanity;

pride. All this stuff didn't mean anything. It was like vapor quickly passing away like our lives. Our lives are like a vapor; here today, gone tomorrow and only temporary, passing away quickly. The material things of this world do not really mean anything. Because our father is rich in houses and land, he holds the power of the world in his hands. So if you desire or need something, ask your father, God. You need to *seek ye first the kingdom of God and His righteousness and all of these things shall be added unto you.* What things, everything that you need in this life to survive.

Concerning the rich people, there is still a void within their soul, which they haven't yet realized because they have been trying to fill it with other things. Some are alone in their mansion they'd like to call a home, but instead it's just a house. They turn to drugs to numb the pain, and keep in mind that drugs can kill you. Have you ever watched the news and noticed how a lot of celebrities have overdosed on drugs, losing their lives to have fun, while attempting to numb the pain? I'm sure they weren't thinking about their mansion, or their money in the bank, then.

People turn to alcohol to soothe the pain, and when they are influenced by the alcohol, it takes them to another place (not in their right mind), that brings them back in the morning with nausea, headache and a hangover. Proverbs 23:31-35 says it like this: *"Look not thou upon the wine when it is red, when it gives its color in the cup. In the end it bites like a serpent, and stings like an adder. Your eyes will behold strange things, and your heart will utter perverse things. You will be as he that lie down in the midst of the sea, or as he that lie on the top of a mast. They have stricken me and I was not sick; they have beaten me, and I did not feel it. When shall I awake so I can seek out another drink?"*

So why would anyone drink to get drunk if it has this kind of affect on them? Why would you want to lose your mind? To answer that question as simply as possible, something is missing and that something is God. Again, nothing can satisfy the longing in their soul but God. People turn to alcohol and so many other things to gratify the flesh, but it is the soul that needs to be catered to, fed, and taken care of more than the flesh. If your soul is whole and you are feeding your spirit with the Word, prayer and worship, you can control the flesh. *Walk in the spirit and you will not fulfill the lusts of the flesh. (Read Galatians 5:19-21 regarding the lusts of the flesh and check all that apply.)* All the money in the world won't satisfy. Nor all the men or women, or, dare I say the forbidden word, sex. Yes, even all the sex you get in the world won't satisfy you, neither food, or mansions, or any other earthly thing. Nothing will ever completely satisfy you because only Jesus Christ can *totally* satisfy you. I believe when God created you, He left a hole within your soul that only He could fill.

That's why everything else you do leaves you unsatisfied. Don't you get it? How many times do I have to say it? There is a spiritual yearning in every soul wanting to know God. Whether they admit it or not, they need Him. They turn to the psychics or astrologers looking for answers, but still can't find them. Why not try Jesus? What do you have to lose? You have nothing to lose but everything to gain. If you lose your life in Christ you can't find it except you come through him to find it. Your life is hid in Christ. Get it? The bottom line is you need Jesus. We need Jesus. As a matter of fact, we all need him. And yes, even you, the doubter, the one who will not believe because of traditional religious belief. You need him too. We can't make it without him. We can't breathe without him. We can't move without Him. We can't live without Him. *It is in Him that we live, move and have our being.*

Taliah didn't realize that Jesus was the only one that could satisfy her until she entered her wilderness. Money wasn't the problem, although she didn't have much, she was able to survive. Her problem was men. She turned to six different men trying to satisfy the longing within the depths of her soul. But she still was left empty and unsatisfied, thirsting for their love.

She was codependent. She depended on men for her happiness. She thinks the men in her life are the only ones that could make her happy, and satisfy her thirsty desires. As she is walking in the desert, her mouth is dry and she needs some water to quench her thirst and refresh her flesh. But what she really needs is water for her soul that will quench all other thirsts. Her journey in the wilderness begins when she starts searching for love in all the wrong faces: men.

Chapter Four

Husband #1

The Adulterer
Searching For Love
In All The Wrong Faces

Proverbs 6:32
   "But whoever committeth adultery with a woman lacketh understanding: he that doeth it destroyeth his own soul."

Taliah is on her way to the well to draw fresh water. With her bucket swinging in her hand, anxious to draw water, Taliah ponders in her mind why it is so hard for men to love her. She wonders what she has done to continue to get rejected and mistreated. She thinks about all the bad relationships she has been in: man after man, husband after husband, and live-in boyfriends. She has been married and divorced five times, and now she is living with the sixth man. She has been searching for love in all the wrong faces. Taliah thinks back to her first husband, Brian. Brian was a loving, charming, and handsome man, who took care of his family. Women loved him because of his good looks. Taliah was blessed to have been chosen by this man. There was only one problem: he was too good looking and he knew it. He was a player before he married Taliah.

He loved a variety of women, and they loved him. They flaunted themselves around him all the time. They didn't care that he was married now. But Brian cared, especially in the beginning stages of their marriage. He respected Taliah as his wife. He made it very clear to the other women that he was happily married to a beautiful woman.

Taliah gave him exactly what he wanted. She felt she

fulfilled his desires and all of his needs as a wife. She cooked for him, served him, kept the house clean, folded and ironed his clothes and helped him the best way she could. She was what you would call a true "help meet." *Women nowadays don't do all that. Where are all the Proverbs 31 women?* However, she knew she wasn't the perfect wife, but she tried to give her best. Of course, he thought otherwise. Obviously her best wasn't good enough. Taliah realized this, and felt Brian should have realized it as well before writing her a certificate of divorce.

She still doesn't understand what went wrong. He seemed to be the perfect husband. He was handsome, charming, and gentle. He paid her compliments, brought her flowers, showed her affection daily and made passionate love to her at night. She thought he was God sent. But after a year of marriage, she started to notice that he began to change. The flowers stopped. The compliments stopped. He no longer paid her any attention or gave her the affection she desired. Brian stopped communicating with her. He didn't make love to her anymore. Then he started coming home late from work. Before, he could hardly wait to get home to eat the dinner she so eagerly and lovingly prepared for him. Now, he would come home late, miss dinner and then would leave early before breakfast.

"He must think I'm stupid," Taliah thought. "He's got to be seeing someone else. I know he had a problem with women when we first got married, but he told me when we were dating that only I could settle him down. I was the only one for him. He let all the other women go for me."

Taliah felt so flattered by his conniving words. *Taliah, come on! Give me a break girl! Don't be so naïve. You should have known better than to marry this man. He wasn't ready to settle down.*

She cooked for him and had it ready for him when he walked in the door. She would make sure she was presentable, smelled good, her makeup was flawless and she was fixed up nicely. She didn't have to do too much, because she was a naturally beautiful woman. Men were always very attracted to her. But then one night, Brian didn't come home. She worried that something had happened to him. Where on earth could he be? She stayed up all night wondering, tossing and turning. Her body finally gave up the fight and she fell asleep on the couch. A door slam woke her up hours later. It was morning, and her husband was home. Taliah said to Brian, "Where have you been? I was worried sick about you. Did something happen? Are you alright?"

"Yes Taliah, I'm alright. I just needed some time to myself away from home to think about a few things."

"Well, why didn't you just tell me? I've been up all night worried sick about you, thinking some wild animal attacked you."

"Well, I'm sorry; I really didn't mean to worry you. But listen, I am not trying to make this long and drawn out, but I need to talk to you about something."

"Okay, I'm listening. What is it Brian?" Taliah was concerned.

"Well, I really don't know how to tell you this, so I'm just going to come out and say it. I no longer want to be married to you."

"What?"

"I no longer want to be married to you. I am writing a certificate of divorce."

"What?"

"I just don't have any interest in you anymore. Our marriage has run its course. It has grown cold."

"Cold? What do you mean cold? You think I'm stupid don't you?" *Uh oh. She feels the tears and the knot forming in her throat.* "You are seeing somebody else aren't you?"

"To be honest with you, yes I am, and I'm leaving you for her. Sorry it has to be this way Taliah and I should have told you a long time ago, but hey, things happen."

"How could you be so cold and so blunt? I love you

with all of my heart. I gave you my heart. Why do you wish to break it when I freely gave it to you? I did everything to try to please you. I gave you my best, but I guess my best wasn't good enough was it?" *The tears were pouring now. Poor Taliah.* "Brian, how could you? Don't you still love me?"

"Look, I said I'm sorry, and there really is nothing more to say. It's over. I am going back out. I just came home to get a few things for the week. I will be back in a couple of days. And when I come back, please don't be here. I want you out of my house."

"Out of your house? This is our house! Where am I going to go?" She pauses. "And where are you going now? Are you going to her house?"

"Well, that's not any of your business now is it?"

"I'm still your wife Brian; you can at least respect me. Who is she? Tell me Brian, who is she?"

"Look I told you, it's none of your business and I don't want to talk about this anymore. It's over. I'm leaving."

"But Brian, where am I supposed to go?"

"You can go back to your family. I'm sure somebody else will marry you. You are a very attractive woman. You don't have a problem getting a man; you just have a problem keeping him."

"A problem keeping him? What is that supposed to mean?"

"Look, I told you it's over and that's all you need to know. Goodbye Taliah." Brian walks out the door and Taliah begins to cry uncontrollably. She can't believe this was happening to her. She wondered how he could just leave like that. Didn't he still love her? What did she do to deserve this?

She picks up an old picture of them together that was sitting on the table and throws it at the door, breaking it into pieces, and continues to cry. She asks herself what went wrong. She knew she wasn't perfect; she had her flaws just like he did. But where did it go wrong? What led him to another woman?

He wasn't supposed to break the covenant. They'd made a vow. How could he cheat on her with another woman? He committed adultery and that is just dead wrong.

This is a good place to take a note. As the scripture says, *whoever committeth adultery with a woman lacketh understanding: he that doeth it destroyeth his own soul.* Don't you know that anyone that commits adultery is committing a sin against God? You don't even understand what you are doing and you are destroying your soul. This type of behavior is unacceptable. I feel sorry and pray for the women that have experienced this. If you are still in a relationship with a husband who committed adultery and your plan is to stay married to him, then you must forgive him and allow God to repair your marriage. Some say, well, I can forgive him but I can't forget. Well then sweetie you really haven't truly forgiven him. If you still want him, ask God to help you to forgive and forget and to help you through the healing and to regain your trust back. And He will do just that. However, if you have left your husband because of adultery and plan to divorce that is acceptable according to scripture. For the only grounds for divorce is adultery. OK; back to Taliah.

Taliah remembered prior to him leaving that he did seem uninterested in her. No longer did he desire her. He expected her to be perfect, but nobody is perfect but God. Reality brings her mind back as she continues walking on her journey. Taliah realized that she wasn't all that spiritual nor did she consider herself to be a Christian. Taliah thought, maybe that's why Brian left, because we were sleeping together before we got married? Maybe God is paying me back for the sins that I committed continuously? God; who is this spiritual being anyway?

She knew a little bit about God. Her father and grandparents taught her about Him as a little girl. She understood clearly God's laws. She thought she understood the oracles of God and the Mosaic Law. Taliah knew that He was and is the creator of the universe and He does exist and she believed in worshipping him. She was taught that her fathers worshipped in the mountains and so she worshipped Him as well, the religious way. However, she really didn't fully understand true worship and who God really was, and didn't know him personally; although she read about him. It really didn't matter to her though now, because he didn't care anything about her. So she thought. She did know that he was a God of love; however, her sinful nature knew He was a God of Judgment and a God of Wrath and she sensed that he probably wanted more from her life.

Yes, Taliah. You're right. God does want more from your life. He wants you to surrender your life to Him. And, God is *way* more than that! God is everything. God is love. God is the Supreme Spiritual Being who is to be worshipped. God is a spirit. For they who worship Him *must worship Him in spirit and in truth.* God is the I am that I am. He is the Jehovah Elohim, our creator. He is your provider, your redeemer, the lover of your soul, your friend, your husband. He is the father, yet the son.

Wow! God's got it going on! He is the Holy Spirit. He is God in flesh; Jesus. He is the Word. *In the beginning was the Word and the Word was with God and the Word was God. The same was in the beginning with God. All things were made by Him and without him wasn't anything made that was made. In him was life and that life was the light of men. And that light shineth in darkness but the darkness comprehended it not.* Wow! God is awesome, isn't He? He is the father, yet the son and the Holy Ghost, and *these three are one.* Taliah you have no idea who you are about to encounter on your journey. So brace yourself girl, someone is waiting for you at the well. Even though you don't know who He is yet, you will.

Taliah knew God was not pleased with her living with a man right now, and she knew that one day she would have to pay for her sins. Little did she know *God so loved her that He gave His only begotten son, that whosoever believeth in Him should not perish but have everlasting life.* And this same God, in flesh, is waiting for her at the well at the end of her journey, and His grace is covering her, even in the midst of her sin. He just wants her to recognize it. But at this moment, she didn't realize this and didn't really care. As a matter of fact, she didn't care about too much of anything. The people of the town looked at her funny every time she went to the well to draw water.

She could hear the women whispering and saying, "Look at her. There she goes again. She's going to the well to get some water. If I were her, I would be ashamed to even come out with all the men she's been with. Did you hear how many husbands she has had?"

"Husbands? Please, I don't even think they ever married her. They just got what they wanted and sent her on her way."

"Yeah, I heard she was so easy. She will give away her goods to anybody that showed any interest in her."

"She thinks because the men are attracted to her good looks, she can get anybody she wants."

"I don't know who she thinks she is. She is pretty but she's not all that, taking all the men in our town. We have it hard trying to get one for ourselves. And she has had I think seven or eight or maybe ten! And wait . . . isn't she living with somebody now?"

"She ain't nothing but the devil himself in a red dress."

She can hear them laughing loudly and mocking her.

This is a good place to take a note. People should not worry about what people say or think of them. Most of the rumors and gossip that people say aren't even true. So since you know that and you know who you are and *whose* you are, you should never let people bring you down. Do not seek their approval, but seek the approval of God. Don't worry, but *cast all your cares (concerns and worries) upon Him because he cares for you.* Like a father cares for his natural daughter, so does your father God care for you. And whenever the enemies are talking about you and gossiping behind your back, let God deal with them. They are just envious anyway.

Every time Taliah went out to draw water from the well, they stared at her - whispering, laughing and saying bad things about her. They were just *busy bodies and backbiters*. "Why are they whispering? They don't even know me," she thought! "Do they think I enjoy living like this? I am not a prostitute, and I'm sure that is what they think I am. I am just a woman that needs a little love, and they should quit acting like they're any better than me because I'm sure they have had their share of men too. I may be sharing my bed with a man now, but I was married five times before. At least I had husbands and not boyfriends." *Taliah what are you saying girl?*

The more she thought about how she was used in the past by her previous' husbands, tears began to flood her eyes and a knot formed in her stomach making her feel like she was going to throw up. She looked down at the jewelry around her ankle that her first husband Brian made for her. She knelt down as the tears were dropping from her eyes and out of anger and hurt, yanked the gold jewelry from around her ankle, breaking it and throwing it. Then she took the gold ring out of her nose and threw it and thought I don't need any of this. She sat down on the hot sand in the desert and put her head down and folded her arms on top of her knees and began to sob bitterly and uncontrollably. She was severely depressed. She had no confidence in herself. She lost what little self-esteem she had.

After she was done releasing her tears, she came to herself and decided what is done is done. I will live my life the way that I want. This is my life and I will live it the way I choose. I know I have made some bad choices, but I guess I have to live with the choices I made. *This is a good place for a quick note. Choose ye this day whom you will serve!* Will it be God or man? Women let me tell you something. When you are feeling down and out, and when you are severely depressed, cry out to God and read the book of Psalms. Memorize the scriptures. Meditate on them. I personally love Psalm 42. The

Psalmist David said, "*why art thou disquieted in me? hope thou in God.*" Sometimes you have to talk to yourself and say, "Self, hey, get it together." Don't let your emotions get the best of you. Don't let your flesh control your spirit. *Walk in the spirit and you will not fulfill the lusts of the flesh.*

A lot of times and quite often, women react out of their flesh when they are emotional. They are not thinking rationally and make big mistakes and bad choices as well as bad decisions. Their mouth sometimes is uncontrollable, they say things to hurt others and develop a vengeful spirit, which is not of God. Your mouth can lead to sin. *In the multitude of words sin is not absent. The tongue is evil; no man can tame it and is set on fire by hell.* Do you ever wonder why when you start yapping you can't stop? It's because your flesh has taken over. You need to be quiet, and give your emotions over to God. Allow God's spirit to help you control your emotions and He will because a *meek and quiet spirit is pleasing to Him.* You can also praise and worship your way out of it. As a matter of fact, after you ask God to help you, you need to worship. Praise yourself out of the depression. When you praise and worship God, even in spite of your emotional state, your hurtful feelings and your tears, you will receive deliverance. All of a sudden your spirit is no longer broken. Your spirit has been strengthened. God has sent his angel to minister to you. *God dwells in the midst of your praises.* No longer are you depressed but you have been set free! And this confuses the Devil because he attempts to attack you at the times that you are weak and emotional. We will discuss that more in another chapter.

Anyway, Taliah had become numb to the pain. She was in denial and pretending as though nothing was wrong. She was hiding behind her broken smile as a lot of women do. A lot of women hide behind their careers, their marriages, their makeup, their clothes, their men. Wanting to appear as though they are strong and have there act together. They even hide behind religion and/or church ministries. They get involved in different ministries within the church, sometimes more then they can handle. They use it as a way of escape. They pretend as though everything is okay. But in reality, deep down inside, they are broken and torn little girls locked inside a woman's body, screaming silently inside for someone to come and unlock the door and let her out so she can scream. HELP!!

Taliah had made some bad choices in life and really hasn't yet understood how to make the right choices and didn't have the wisdom to. Her family and what little friends she had, abandoned her and forsook her because of her lifestyle. So Taliah, still searching for love in all the wrong faces, marries her second husband, Douglas.

Chapter Five

Husband #2
The Alcoholic

Ephesians 5:18
"And be not drunk with wine, wherein is excess; but be
filled with the Spirit."

Do you ever wonder why people turn to alcohol when it is bad for them? They love what it can do for them. They love how it makes them feel. It's already bad enough to drink it when it damages your liver and other organs in your body. But to get drunk off of it isn't a good thing. People think a little alcohol won't hurt anybody. Yeah, that's true. However, when you drink one, then two, then three glasses, and you get drunk, it becomes a problem. Why not be filled with the spirit and get drunk in the spirit instead? Do you realize the way you feel after getting drunk from wine, alcohol or whatever your Friday night drink may be? It does not compare to getting drunk in the spirit. That is such a wonderful experience! I encourage you, if you haven't been filled with the spirit of God, speaking in other tongues as the spirit of God gives you utterance, ask God for the gift of the Holy Ghost.

Being filled with the spirit not only empowers you supernaturally, which enables you and gives you power to defeat the enemy when he comes against you, but it takes you to another place in the spiritual realm. We will discuss this in another chapter. God's presence is so real. I'm telling you, He's real. So instead of getting drunk on wine, Hennessey, beer,

Long Island Ice Tea's, Vodka, Tequila, or whatever your drink is, give it up. Get drunk on Jesus. *And be not drunk with wine but be filled with the spirit.* If you are indeed a believer, you need the Holy Spirit who will give you power. Acts 19:2 reads: *"Have ye received the Holy Ghost since ye believed?"* Don't get drunk with wine. Don't become an alcoholic. Be filled with the spirit. I will talk more about this in another chapter. OK . . . now back to Taliah.

As Taliah continued walking, she thought about her second husband, Douglas. Douglas was a short man and kind of boyish looking. But it was something about him that she loved. He was so kind and loving. But there was one problem and it was a problem that she couldn't handle. He was a leach. *Have you ever had a man in your life that was a leach? Pause a minute and think back. You know you did.* He had no job, no money, no means of transportation, nothing. He was (can I say it?) a bum. He was a no good bum and known to be a leach. She didn't understand why he didn't have a job like the other men. He was down right lazy. Proverbs 6:9 says, *how long wilt thou sleep, you sluggard? When will you get up and arise out of your sleep? Yet a little sleep, a little slumber, a little folding of the hands to sleep, so shall poverty come upon you like one that travelleth, and you will want as an armed man.*

Taliah doesn't even understand why she was with this man. She didn't even love him. He wasn't her type. He did nothing for her. He was no good. However, Taliah didn't want to be alone and she was still hurting from her first husband leaving her for another woman. So she promised herself she would marry the next man that showed any interest to help her get through the hurt and pain. She couldn't be alone. She was so lonely and still had open wounds within her that needed to heal. So when she met Douglas, in order to heal her pain, she decided to just replace Brian with Douglas. He would help her forget about Brian. He's someone who would love her. Since Brian was very handsome, she thought if she got someone who wasn't as attractive this time he would never leave her. As a matter of fact, she felt like she was the best thing that had ever happened to Douglas. *Ladies, please don't settle for less because of loneliness. Don't settle for Buckwheat when you can have a Boaz!*

Douglas loved to take her out in the town to show her off. And she enjoyed the attention. It felt good getting attention. But there was only one problem, when they would go out in the town Douglas would run into his buddies and they would all end up drinking wine together and getting drunk. Taliah didn't drink. She would just sit there looking stupid, wanting to have fun, not knowing what to do because she didn't drink. She definitely was not approving of her husband drinking, but she knew there was nothing she could do about it. She talked to him about it at home, but he didn't listen. She tried to take it away, but he thought she was crazy. Taking away Douglas' alcohol was like taking away a bottle of milk from a hungry baby. She really didn't want to be there, but Douglas made her go. He said they were one and he wanted them to always be together everywhere they went. Plus, he enjoyed flaunting her around his friends because he said she was so fine.

This went on and on for several years until one night, when they went out in the town, Douglas had gotten so drunk on wine that he passed out. Taliah didn't know if it was the wine that caused him to pass out, because he had never passed out before. She didn't know wine could have this affect on people. She didn't know what to do. "Somebody get a physician; something is wrong with my husband!"

"Nawh it ain't," one of his friends said, "he's fine. He just had a little too much wine to drink. He'll be alright. Leave him be."

"Why don't you just take him home? You know, since he passed out and all."

"That's nice of you," Taliah said. "It's nice of you to take us home."

"I'm not talking about you dear. I was talking about

your husband."

"Well, why would you take my husband home and not me?"

"We like your company. Why don't you have a drink with us and loosen up a bit? You need a little something to lighten you up," *(laughing and looking at her lustfully)*. Meanwhile, the other man takes Douglas home.

"Why don't you have a drink?" he said.

"No, I don't think so. I don't drink."

"You here that boys? Douglas' wife said she doesn't drink? Well, by the time we get done with her tonight, she will be drinking. As a matter of fact, give her one now," they laughed.

"What are you talking about? It's time for me to go home."

She starts walking away and one of the men grabs her by the arm and says, "You ain't going nowhere, miss pretty thing you. The party is just getting started. Here, drink this." He holds her face and tries to make her drink.

"What are you doing? Stop that! I told you I don't drink. Let go of me!" She knocks the glass of wine out of his hand.

"Oh that's alright. Come on over here to me sugar. I heard you've been around town. How about giving me some of what you got?" He grabs her a little rougher this time.

"Yeah," one of the other men said, "give us all some of what you got. You show look good!" They all surround her; laughing, drunk, and smelling like a bucket of alcohol and dirty sweat.

"You boys better get away from me or I'll scream! I mean it. Leave me alone! I'm married to your friend. How can you disrespect him like that? Please, leave me alone! I need to go home!"

"Lady, you ain't going no where. Come here." He pulls her close to him.

"Stop! What are you doing? Stop!" She slaps him hard

on the face. "I said stop!"

"Now you really got it coming." The man throws her on the ground, hits her, and busts her lip causing her to bleed. Then he rapes her. She screams. She yells. She kicks. She cries. But they block out her pleading cry. They can't hear her and don't care. Each of them took turns, being very rough and doing horrible things. Finally, when all three of them were done doing what they were doing, they left. They left her on the floor . . . in her tears . . . in her blood . . . in her torn clothes . . . in her pain and in her shame.

Taliah got up crying; shaking nervously. She was disturbed and couldn't believe what just happened. She was somewhat numb. All she could think about was getting home and telling Douglas what his so-called friends did to her. She ran home angry, crying, and trying to keep her torn clothes from falling off. When she got home, there was her husband drunk and sleep on the couch. She looked at him briefly, in disgust, then ran past him through the back door of their cabin and jumped in the lake where she began washing and cleaning herself. "No! No! No! No!" She screamed and cried. Her scream woke up Douglas and he ran stumbling, still partially drunk, out the back door.

"Taliah, what's wrong with you? You okay?"

"No I'm not okay. Your so-called friends raped me!"

"What!"

"They raped me. Each one of them." She started crying and wiped the blood off her face. "They were all touching me and taking turns with me. Oh Douglas, they were laughing and calling me names. Then one of them hit me in my face and told me to shut up. Douglas why would they do this? I'm supposed to be their friend's wife and I'm a lady. They are supposed to respect me as a lady. How could they do this to me and to you? They are not friends of yours doing something like that."

Douglas didn't say anything. "Did you hear what I just said? I was just raped by your friends! Douglas? Do you have anything to say about this? What are you going to do about it?"

He grabs her by the arm and pulls her close to him. He had a horrible stench and the alcohol was still strong on his breath. He wasn't completely sober yet, but he said, "I'm going to tell you what I'm going to do about it. Nothing. Absolutely nothing. You are out of here. Get your stuff and get out! I am writing you a certificate of divorce. I don't want you no more. Your body was given to other men, and it does not belong to me anymore."

"What do you mean *given?* Did you hear anything I said? I said they raped me, which means they took it from me. I didn't give them anything. They took it. They took advantage of me Douglas. I didn't give them anything. They took advantage of your wife. They raped me! Don't you care what they did to your wife? I'm your wife! They took something that belonged to you."

"Used to belong to me. But not anymore. You don't belong to me no more. Go get your stuff and get out of my cabin."

"Get out? Where am I supposed to go Douglas?"

"I don't care where you go, just get out of my sight. I have no use for you anymore. Now go get your stuff and get out!"

"But Douglas, I . . ."

"I said get out and don't come back!"

Taliah runs into the cabin crying and starts to pack her bags again. He follows her to make sure that she leaves. When she was finished packing the last thing, he threw her belongings on the ground, shoved her out the door and closed it behind her.

As Taliah fearfully walked through the dark woods, she saw a small cave. She couldn't believe what just happened. She was so tired and cold. She decided to sleep there for the night and go back to the cabin to talk to Douglas in the morning. She figured he must have been out of his mind to say what he said. He was just drunk and by morning he will be sober.

Taliah slept a restless, sleepless night in that cold dark cave. The sounds of the night kept her up. She was scared, cold and alone. She cried herself to sleep. When morning came, she got up and walked to her cabin. As she was approaching the cabin, she heard voices that sounded like men laughing. She opened the door and there they were - the same men that raped her and fondled her with their dirty hands. The same men that tore her clothes off, smacked her, and disrespected her were all in her home with her husband. And her husband, who was supposed to protect her and make her feel safe and loved, was laughing and drinking with them. The men stopped laughing when she entered the door.

"What are you doing back here?" Douglas said. "I thought I told you to not come back."

"Look at her," one of the men said. "All used up. Nobody gonna want you now."

"Douglas! That's them! They are the ones that raped me!" Taliah cried.

"Nobody raped you girl. You gave it up freely. They told me all about it. Men will be men. You just a woman. You have nothing to say about it. And besides, you and I never really connected anyway. I never loved you. I just wanted you for your looks and your body and to say I had a wife."

He said this in front of all the other men. Taliah did not say another word. She ran away with humiliation and cried. She found herself single again; by herself with no one to love her, hold her, wipe her tears away or comfort her. No one could love her the way she deserved to be loved.

Taliah, you poor thing. Oh, you poor thing. If you only knew Jesus? Jesus' love goes beyond the world's kind of love, especially a man's love. Oh, Taliah, if you only knew Jesus.

Chapter Six

Husband #3
The Controller

Ephesians 5:23
> *"For the husband is the head of the wife, even as Christ is the head of the church: and he is the saviour of the body."*

This is the passage of scripture that a lot of husbands get twisted and take out of context. Just because God said you are the head of the wife doesn't mean you should control your wife. Husbands don't need to control their wives in everything they do, treat them as though they're not equal or beneath you because they are *women*. The controlling man is a man that cares nothing about his wife's opinion, feelings, thoughts, goals, dreams, or anything that makes his wife happy. All he wants is control. He wants control over the money, control over the sex *(always his ways, never hers)* control over the communication aspect of the marriage like when she should speak and when she should not speak, control over the kids *(never able to discipline the motherly way, remember God gave a child two parents)*, control over everything.

The wife is unable to be herself, so she keeps everything inside for peace sake. She doesn't realize that burying your emotions and feelings; pretending as though it's okay when it's not; hiding behind a disguised mask and covering it up with Revlon and a broken smile; not being able to vent and release your thoughts; not being able to express the real you the way God created you, which is *fearfully and wonderfully made by*

God, the Creator Himself; unable to talk to your supposed to be companion, which used to be your best friend in the beginning and you could tell him anything *(remember when he use to listen?)*; holding all these things inside and not communicating can cause an explosion one day. Holding things inside is not healthy. You are only human and far from perfect. No one is perfect but God.

The controlling man may not have a temper, but belittles his wife because of his own insecurities. He feels that since he is the head of the house, the king of his castle as they say, God has given him the power. He tweaks the scripture that says, *wives be obedient to your husband in everything and to be subject to your own husband.* So he feels that the wife must always do what he says. He forgets the scripture that reads, *for the husband and the wife are to be subject to one another* and *for husbands to love your wife as Christ loves the church.* Just think of how Christ loves the church. He loves us so much that He gave his life for us. His grace, His tender mercy, His compassion, His unconditional love is amazing. Like so, husbands are to sacrifice their lives and love their wives in the same way, not controlling them. They are fragile and can easily break, and need to be cherished, nurtured, spoken tenderly to, and loved. Controlling husbands don't do that. Anyway, Taliah experienced this type of man. She meets and married her third husband, which so happens to be that controlling man.

Taliah meets Mark in the park three months later. *Taliah you should have allowed yourself time to heal from your previous marriage.* She marries him within five months. She couldn't help herself. Mark was a charmer. He was very good looking and a perfect gentleman. He listened to her. He made her feel like she was everything. She thought she'd finally married someone who would be good to her. But she really didn't know Mark. Mark had some issues in his life that he hadn't dealt with yet. He never acknowledged that he had any issues. He thought he was God's gift to women.

This is a good place to take a note. First of all, Taliah didn't allow herself time to heal from the previous marriage, and she appears to be a little desperate. She married Mark with her unhealed wounds and out of her desperation to be loved by a man, any man. It didn't matter as long as she had a man. *Taliah you sound desperate girl. Slow down!* She didn't even know him that well. She thought she knew him, but she didn't really know the real Mark. She didn't give herself time to get to know him, and she never sought God about him. Come to think of it, Taliah never asked God about any of the men that she married. Taliah didn't have a relationship with God. But if you do, woman of God who is reading this book, and if you are single, you better pray to God every time about any man that you meet and date. Ask the Holy Spirit to give you wisdom and spiritual discernment so you will know if this man is a man of God. As a matter of fact, pray and ask God to bring only who He wants you to have. This will save you a lot of headache and heartache.

And ladies, you have to allow time to get to know someone and time to heal before jumping into another relationship. It doesn't matter how wonderful it feels to have a man take you out, dress up for, pay you compliments, buy you gifts, or make you feel like a lady. Don't rush it. Enjoy the dating season. Why are you in a hurry? I know you felt a wonderful feeling as though you've known him forever. It's supposed to feel that way in the beginning. You both have your best foot forward. Enjoy him. Let him take you out for a while.

Often women make decisions out of their own emotional state, as I mentioned in the previous chapter. Taliah was broken, rejected and feeling lonely. She wanted love so badly that she turned to another man to try to help her get through the pain from her previous husband. And she didn't like being alone. I think most people don't like to be alone, because God created us to enjoy each other. Remember Adam and Eve? God said *it was not good for man to be alone, so I will make him a helper.* He made woman for the man and they became one flesh. Even so, you don't have to be with everybody and anybody because of feeling lonely. Wait for God and He will send you someone that He has created just for you.

Taliah was beautiful and never had any problems getting a man because of her looks. But once she got them, she couldn't keep them because she was so damaged inside. They took advantage of her insecurities, her desperation to be loved, and her vulnerability. She was naive and gullible and they really took her for granted.

About a year later, Taliah was taking a nap in the middle of the day when she heard Mark come in. She got up quickly and tried to clean up the house. "What is he doing home so early?" She thought. She was so tired, she fell asleep and didn't get the chance to fix dinner or clean up. She knew how he loved to come home to a clean house and dinner ready as soon as he walked in the door. She didn't expect him until dinner time. She ran up to him, kissed him and said, "Hi honey, how was your day?"

"My day was doing fine until I came home to see this house a mess."

"Oh honey, I'm sorry. I fell asleep."

"Yeah, okay whatever. Where's my dinner?"

"Well, I haven't had a chance to fix your dinner yet because I fell asleep. Besides, you are home early. What are you doing home so early?"

"What are you doing sleeping in the middle of the day? Look at you. You look a mess. Look at this house."

"I said I was sorry. I promise I will make it up to you. Now what would you like for dinner?"

"Doesn't matter. Just fix me something quick. I'm starving."

"Okay. I will. But can I have some sugar first?" She walks over to give him a passionate kiss and get a big bear hug, but he pushes her away.

"Mark, all I want is a little affection."

"Look, I told you I am not the affectionate type, so stop trying to get me to give you affection. I will give you sex only when I want it or need it."

"But Mark, I'm not talking about sex. I just need a little affection. You were so affectionate in the first six months of our marriage. What happened? Do you still find me attractive?" She walks over to him again, puts her arms around his chest and kisses him gently on his neck. He pushes her away again and says,

"Look, I told you to stop that. I done told you over and over again I am not affectionate. Now stop all this affectionate talk and go fix me something to eat."

As she walks over to put his dinner on, she says, "Mark, seriously, I really need to talk about this affection issue and every time I bring up the topic you shut me down. I told you before we got married that I was a very affectionate woman. Don't you believe that in order to have a lasting, loving and fulfilling marriage, a couple has to compromise? I understand you didn't receive much affection in your childhood, but I know it's in you. You were so affectionate in the beginning and I know you can give it if you wanted to. You want affection too, in your own way, and you get it one way or the other, but I don't. I . . ."

"Look, I am going to say this one final time I am not an affectionate person. My mother and father weren't affectionate. Affection wasn't in my home."

"I understand that, but just because you didn't receive affection that doesn't mean you can't give it? Affection is a way a person expresses their love to another, and I am a woman that needs affection."

This is a good place to take a note. If there are any men reading this, listen up. The Bible says to *render the affection that is due unto her*. Women need affection. It really doesn't matter if you are affectionate or not. You need to compromise and give your wife affection at least sometimes. You really need to give her the affection that is due unto her as it says in God's Word. God created a woman to want affection. When a woman receives affection, it makes her feel loved, desired and wanted. And while you're at it, pay her compliments, take her out on a date, buy her flowers, and spend some quality time with her.

When a man does this to a woman, it unlocks her womanhood. As a matter of fact, husbands can get what they want more easily if they love their wives this way. *Husbands love your wife as Christ loves the church and gave him self for her.* So as you love her, and compromise with sacrifice by giving up yourself for her, she won't have a problem submitting to you. Although wives, you must submit, honor, obey and reverence your husband regardless if he is rendering affection or not. However, submit only as he submits to Christ. If he tells you to jump off the cliff, are you going to jump? I think not. You cannot obey or follow him if he is not following Christ. If He is going against God's will and the Word of God, he's not following Christ. Okay; back to Taliah.

"Just fix my dinner please. I am tired of hearing about this."

"Honey, I really wish we would communicate more. Communication is important and I think . . ."

"Would you just shut up! Please? I don't want to talk about this anymore. Can I just have some peace? I didn't come home from work for this. Can a man get some peace around here?"

Taliah had so much to say, but she didn't say another word. She stopped talking about anything to her husband. She didn't like the tone of voice he used. She didn't like him yelling at her. So she kept her thoughts, feelings and the inability to express herself inside. Months went by with no communication and no affection. At night, sometimes, she wished Mark would reach out for her and just hold her tightly. Because she was emotionally detached from him now, she didn't care if he did or not. She was beginning to lose interest. But still, as a woman, she still yearned to be held by her husband.

So there they lay in the same bed, in the same house, in the same room, but living separate lives everyday. He went his way and she went hers. Nobody cared, and nobody dared to talk about their feelings. She wanted to, but she knew it wouldn't do any good. She would just sound like a broken record repeating herself over and over again. She couldn't talk, couldn't express herself, and couldn't address issues or the problems in their marriage because if she did, he would just say she was nagging or fussing. She merely wanted to be heard. She wanted to talk, laugh, play, and express how she really felt inside beneath her heartache and the tears that wet her pillow at night.

He was supposed to be there for her. He promised to love her and cherish her. He made a vow. They were now one. Well they were supposed to be. Now she finds herself living with a stranger from a distant land, someone she thought she knew. She watches him on the other side of the room, sitting there cold as ice not even noticing her. She still wanted him to open up and talk to her, but she knew he never would. She felt the tension so strong and thick in the air. She desperately wanted to tell him how she really felt about everything, but she knew he wouldn't listen. Why would he, he never have before? She even wrote long letters to express how she felt. But she doesn't know if he ever took the time to read them or not because he never responded. There was no communication, just dinner and silence, which eventually became both their companions.

Wives, please, if you are married to a controlling man, know that talking, nagging, and fussing, is not going to make him do anything different. Your best and only solution is to pray. You must pray for your husband everyday. God can do the impossible. God can change him, or change you. You must pray and ask God to give you the strength to help you through this. God knows your desires, your needs, and your wants. He sees your tears, concerns, and worries so take it all to the Lord and tell Him everything. *Cast all of your cares upon him because he cares for you.* Beloved, tell Him what you need and either God will give you the strength to deal with him or change him. But in Taliah's case, she didn't know Jesus, so there wasn't much she could do to save her marriage.

Finally, after three months, Mark broke the silence and said, "Taliah, I don't want this marriage anymore. I'm writing you a certificate of divorce."

This time Taliah spoke and let it all out. After months of build up, she said, "Fine. Whatever you want as long as you are happy. It's obvious that you are not happy because you haven't touched me in months. You haven't talked to me yet. You talk to everybody else. You haven't spent any quality time with me or taken me out like you use too. We don't talk anymore about anything. We used to laugh and play and show love to each other. Now there's nothing, so you don't care if I am here or not. You wanted to control everything that I did, yet it is so difficult for you to love me the way that I deserve to be loved.

"Mark, I know that you may have loved me in your own way, but you were unable to love me the way that I want to be loved. I have so much love to give away that I'm about to explode. I need to give it away. I need to give it to someone who will appreciate it and who can give it back to me. It's obvious that you can't and won't give me what I need. You have made it very clear. So if you don't want me anymore, that's fine. I will leave." *Taliah if you have that much love to give, and if you only knew Jesus you could of given that love away to others who need it more then you do.*

Finally, the build up for months had been released. It wasn't all of it, but it was some of it. She had so much more to say, but why say anything else? He told her he didn't want her anymore, so she walks to her bedroom and starts packing her clothes. As the tears begin to fall hard, she thinks how packing and unpacking is becoming a lifestyle. In the last few years, she has moved and packed quite often. She was sick and tired of it and asked God, "Where are you in all of this, and why do you keep allowing me to get hurt over and over and over again." She wondered if God had any man out there who would treat her with love, honor and respect. Taliah catches herself. "I know I'm not talking to God again. He doesn't care about me. Besides, He's not even listening. Just like He didn't listen the first time."

She continues to pack. *"Taliah."*

"What? Who said that? Mark is that you?" She stops. Although she's unsure of what voice she heard, she knows she heard a voice. Taliah walks out the door with her bags in hand. She doesn't look at Mark because she doesn't want him to see her crying. But she felt him looking at her and thought maybe what she was feeling was his love for her not really wanting her to go. She hoped he would stop her from leaving, take her bags out of her hands, hold her and tell her how much he loved her. She wanted him to say he really didn't want her to go and that he was just angry when he said it. Did he feel anything for her? Did he even care she was leaving? He said nothing; not even a word of goodbye. There was no hug or kiss, or an "I'm sorry; I'll do better." There was no "I don't want you to go." There was nothing but a cold, hard heart that was unreachable.

Well, that was to be expected from him, the controller. He was the most stubborn and coldest of them all. He did a good job hiding this when they were dating. He was totally different then, but now his true identity has made itself known, the controller. He wanted control over everything like what she wore, ate, how she looked, her money and who her friends were. He controlled when she talked. She didn't know when to talk and what to say, because of the response she would get from him. She felt like she was in prison. It was never a pleasant one. He was always so negative about everything. He never had anything good to say to her or about her.

She wondered why and what she did to cause this. When did things start going wrong? It had been so long she couldn't even remember. "He was unhealthy for me anyway," she thought. "Why would I want to be with someone who doesn't want to be with me? So I'm glad it's over. I'm getting use to being alone. However, I still wonder, why I keeping choosing the wrong men?" Just when Taliah thinks she is through with men, she meets her fourth husband, Tyrone, five months later, after Mark divorced her.

Chapter Seven

Husband #4
Sodom & Gomorrah

Romans 1:27
". . . And likewise also the men, leaving the natural use of the woman, burned in their lust one toward another; men with men working that which is unseemly, and receiving in themselves that recompense of their error which was meet."

"Hi honey I'm home!" Tyrone came in eager to see his wife, Taliah.

"Over here. I'm in the kitchen cooking your favorite meal."

"Hey baby. How you doing?" He gives her a hug. "I got something for you." He pulls out a dozen peach roses.

"Oh Tyrone! They're beautiful. Thank you. I will just put these in some water."

"They are beautiful just like my beautiful wife. I can't believe God done blessed me with somebody like you. I don't know what your other husbands were thinking when they let you go. You are a fine woman. And when you get done, I'm going to show you just how much."

"Yeah right, I don't know about that, I've been waiting for you to show up for a while now, however, I don't want any babies. Although it has been a while," Taliah laughed.

"Who said anything about babies?"

"Well if you talking about what I think you are talking about it, that is how you make babies."

Taliah and Tyrone laughed and sat down to a nice dinner. They talked about everything and anything like they had been best friends since high school. They were laughing and having a good time until Tyrone's phone rang.

"Excuse me honey, I got to get this. Hello . . ."

"Oh okay, go ahead honey." Taliah continued to eat dinner. She thought about how glad she was that she married Tyrone. She finally had a man who loved her the way she deserved to be loved. She finally had a man that understood her and listened to her; a man that gave her all the affection she needed. He was almost too good to be true. It has been six months now since they have been married, and they hadn't had one argument. "He is so good to me," Taliah thought. "He's nothing like my previous husbands who didn't know how to treat a lady. When he gets off the phone, I have to show him just how much he means to me. It has been such a long time since we made love.

He's been so busy at work. I need him so badly. He's probably talking to one of his work buddies. Tyrone's a good man; I'm not going to let this one slip away. I will do everything I can to keep him. What are some extra things I can do to keep him? I don't know what more I can do. I am a good wife, as I've always been. I will just make love to him as often as I can so he won't want anybody else. But lately he hasn't wanted it. I wonder why? I guess he's been so tired from working so hard. However, he did mention it at dinner. Anyway, I will try to be submissive. I will support him in all that he does. I will keep myself looking nice. I will keep the house clean. I will love him hard, yet softly, with all of my heart."

While Taliah thought on these *I wills*, Tyrone was hanging up from his phone call. Taliah walked over to him and said, "Hey baby, let's finish our dinner. Then we can have dessert in the bedroom."

"Oh baby, I'm sorry. I'm so sorry. I got a very important phone call so I have to go. I'll be back home in a little while."

Taliah dared not say anything. She didn't want to mess up what they had going. She wanted to ask about the dinner she worked so hard to make, and who it was he was talking to on the phone that interfered with their night. She wanted to know where he was going and why. But, she knew if she asked, it might cause him to think she doesn't trust him or was badgering him. She didn't want him to think she was insecure. So all she said was, "Oh, okay honey; I understand. Just hurry back, okay?"

"I will. Just make sure you wait up for me, ya hear?"

"Okay baby. I'll be waiting for you," she said seductively. Tyrone headed out into the night.

Taliah dozed off to sleep while she was waiting for Tyrone to come home. Before she laid down, she took a nice, hot bubble bath with candles, perfumed her body, and put on some nice smelling fragrance and a lacy white gown. She was waiting anxiously for her husband to come home. It was now around 4:00 in the morning and still no Tyrone. "Where on earth could he be?" she thought as she sat up in her bed. She started to worry and got up to look out the window for him. "Where is he? What is he doing? Why hasn't he come home? He has never done this before. I hope he's alright."

There's nothing she can do now but go back to sleep. She was so tired that she just closed her eyes and fell right back asleep. She tossed and turned in the sheets thinking of how she needed to be held by her husband tonight. She really needed him and her body really needed him, but he wasn't there.

The next morning when Taliah awoke, there was still no Tyrone. She was worried now. She put on her robe and made some breakfast. As she was pouring some cereal in a bowl, she heard someone coming. "Oh good!" Taliah thought. "It's Tyrone." She ran to fix her hair and brush her teeth, only to knock over the box of cereal on the floor. There was no time to clean it up; she wanted to look beautiful for her husband when he walked through the door. *Taliah you are going a little overboard aren't you?* Tyrone comes in.

"Tyrone is that you? I have been worried sick about you. Is everything okay?"

"Hey baby!" He gives her a kiss on the cheek. "What's the cereal doing all over the floor?"

"Oh I just knocked it over. I'll get it up."

"Uh, leave the cereal for now. We need to talk."

"Oh no, here we go again," she thought. She was desperately trying hard not to let her true emotions show such as anger and hurt. Neither did she want to ask the questions that pondered and lingered in her mind like, "Where have you been and who were you with last night?" So instead she simply said, "Okay, sure, what do we need to talk to me about?" Tyrone sits her down on the couch and holds her hands.

"You know I love you right?"

"Yes. I know that without a doubt, Honey. You have showed me how much you love me in so many ways, like the way you look at me, the affection you give to me, the way you make me laugh, the way . . ."

"Taliah, slow down please. I need to tell you something. This is kind of hard for me because I'm just coming to this realization myself. I've been struggling with this for so long. I really didn't have anyone to talk to about it. I'm a little embarrassed, but I have to tell you the truth."

Taliah is nervous now, "Tell me what? Would you please just spit it out?"

"Well Taliah, I do love you but . . . but . . ." Tyrone hesitates.

"But what?"

"I am in love with someone else."

"What! What do you mean someone else?"

"Well it's not what you think. I was seeing Bob before I married you and . . ."

"What? What did you say her name was?"

"Well actually, it's not a her, it's a him."

"A him?"

"Yeah, and his name is Bob. Taliah listen, I will tell you the whole story. Ever since I was a little boy, I have been struggling with my identity. My friends in school always called me a faggot or said I was gay. I was always in denial. But as I grew into a young man, I started developing funny feelings for men. I liked being around them. In high school, girls would never go out with me. I tried to date them, but they just kept on rejecting me. I started hanging out with the guys, and we would go to the clubs and stuff. One thing led to another, and ever since I've been on the down low. I think I got married just to cover up the fact that I am gay. Yeah I said it. I am gay. I used to think I was bisexual, but I know now that I'm gay for sure. I was born gay."

This is a good place to take a note. I don't believe anyone is born gay. God created male and female - Adam and Eve, not Adam and Steve. That's sick. It's not normal and I don't care how many people think that it is okay. It's not, according to scripture and besides, how could a man be with another man? What causes men to turn to men? That is disgusting. And I'm sorry gay men and lesbian women. If you are this way, you are under attack by the enemy. This was not God's original plan. This is unnatural. As it says in Romans 1:27, *likewise also the men, leaving the natural use of the woman, burned in their lust one toward another; men with men working that which is unseemly (meaning, inappropriate, rude, improper, bad-manner), and receiving in themselves that recompense of their error.* Satan has taken over your mind and he is trying to justify what you are doing. It's not okay.

It's wrong. It's dead wrong. You see what happened to the city of Sodom and Gomorrah, which consisted of a lot of gay men? God destroyed that city with fire because of all the sick, disgusting, sexual sins that were in it. So stop it; stop sinning. Get right with God. He loves you. Nothing is impossible through Jesus Christ.

Anyway, Tyrone finishes his story. "The call I got last night was from Bob and he needed to see me. He can't stand being away from me anymore and I just had to go see him." Taliah was speechless, her tongue went numb. "Taliah, please, say something. Listen, you have to believe I still love you and never meant to hurt you. But I can't pretend anymore. I am in love with a man, and I want to be with him. Taliah, do you remember all those nights that I didn't and couldn't make love to you? It's because I wasn't really interested in sleeping with you anymore. I desired a different type of, well you know, a different type of thing. When I realized that I was in love with Bob, and wanted to be with him, there was nothing you could do to turn me on again. So now, if you don't mind, I would like a divorce.

Now, please don't take it personally. You have been a very good wife and everything. You are so beautiful, and I really hate breaking your heart. I know you believed in me and I feel so bad. But I can't and just won't live like this anymore. I don't want to hurt you any more than I already have but I'm tired of pretending. Please try to understand. I know you probably need some time by yourself, so I am going to leave for a few days. OK? Taliah, I am so sorry. I never meant to hurt you. I really did love you and still do."

He walks over to give her a hug, but she says, "No. Don't ever touch me again. Get out of here, just leave. You didn't love me; you don't even know what true love is? *Neither do you, Taliah.* All these months went by and you led me on! How long before the truth came out Tyrone, how long?"

"Taliah, I uh . . ."

"Just shut up! Shut up!! I can't bear to listen to another word of this sick, twisted mess. I'm about to throw up. You make me sick! How could you do something like this? You are disgusting. How can you want another man? What can he do for you that I can't? Well, at least now I know why you haven't been making love to me over the past few months."

"Taliah, I uh . . . I mean, I really tried to uh . . ."

Taliah starts to cry and yells, "Shut up! Just shut up Tyrone. Get out! I said get out now!!!!" Tyrone leaves. She picks up a vase and throws it at the door after Tyrone shuts it.

There . . . Taliah sat, by herself again. She was alone with her thoughts, her tears and her piles of questions asking why, how, when, where? She wondered why she kept getting herself in these situations. Why can't she make better choices in men? Taliah keeps setting herself up to get hurt over and over again. She just can't get the picture. She will never find love until she finds God, for God is love. Taliah continues her search for love in all the wrong faces . . . again.

Chapter Eight

Husband #5
The Abuser

Psalm 58:2
"Yea, in heart ye work wickedness; ye weigh the violence of your hands in the earth."

Six months later, Taliah is at it again. She meets Mr. Rob Foley. Mr. Rob Foley was a very wealthy man and a little older than she. He had himself together, but he was plain and ordinary looking. But there was something about him that made him attractive. However, she had made up her mind six months ago that she was going to just focus on herself, get a job, take care of herself, and enjoy the single life. But then she met Mr. Rob Foley. She met him one day when she was getting some vegetables to make herself a good 'ole dinner.

"Well hello lovely lady, how you doing?" It had been a while since Taliah had spoken to a man because of her previous marriage with Tyrone. She still hadn't gotten over him. She really did love him with her whole heart. He was never really mean to her like the other husbands. He just liked men. She just can't get that out of her mind. How can another man want another man? That is disgusting. Well anyway, that was six months ago and it was time for her to move on. So she responded to Mr. Foley. "I'm doing fine and how are you?"

"I'm doing just fine now that I have met you. May I ask, what is your name?"

"My name is Taliah."

"Well that is a beautiful name. Where did you get a name like that?"

"That's a silly question. I guess my father named me."

"Well he named you well. My name is Rob. They call me Mr. Rob Foley."

"Hello Mr. Rob Foley. It's a pleasure to meet you. But I need to be getting on home now so I can start my vegetables."

"You cookin' dinner or something."

"Yes, I'm cooking dinner this evening."

"Well, what you cooking."

"Why you wanna know?"

"Just asking, that's all."

"Well now, let's see. I have here some potatoes, corn, green beans, fresh fish and some hot cakes for dessert."

"Now Ms. Taliah, stop right there, cause whether you invite me over or not, I'm inviting myself. I haven't had a home cooked meal like that in years, and that's sounding mighty good! Can you make enough for two, I mean including me that is?"

"Oh, I'm sorry. I just assumed you were by yourself. Do you have a family you're cooking for, like a husband and a couple of kids or something?"

"No. No husband and no kids. I just found out I'm barren." *She hesitated.* "I can't have kids. There was one time that I had hoped I'd have a child one day to love and love me back, but it never happened. I went to the doctor, and they discovered after much testing that I was barren." Taliah looks down thinking about what she just said. "Oh, I'm sorry. I didn't mean to just ramble on. Listen to me, opening myself up to a stranger. I don't even know you."

"That's quite alright. I'm all ears. People say I'm a good listener. Besides, I want you to know me and I can't wait to get to know you. If you don't mind, if you would like some company, I'd love to come over for dinner tonight; if you'd invite me."

"Well, that's kinda forward now, isn't it Mr. Foley? Here it is you just met me, and you are inviting yourself over to my place for dinner. I don't even know you. You could be a murderer.

Nope. I don't think so. I am not trying to date anybody and you appear to be a little desperate." "Yeah, I know. So if you say no, I understand. Maybe another time. But ma'am, I am not a murderer. I am one of the nicest men you'll know. I can assure you of that."

Taliah thought to herself, *"No? Are you kidding? It's been so long since I have been around a man and I would love to have him over for dinner and perhaps even spend the night. I need someone and I have been so lonely lately, and oh, if I could . . ."* So she said, "Well okay. I guess it would be alright. You can come by around seven o'clock and be on time. I will be serving dinner right at around seven."

"Oh I wouldn't miss it for the world. Now where's your place?"

"It's just around the corner. Here's my address." She writes down her address and phone number and hands it to him.

"Okay, I will be there right around seven or earlier. I am looking forward to seeing you."

"Okay. See you later, Mr. Foley."

"Alright now, Ms. Lovely, I will most definitely be seeing you later."

Taliah hurries home to clean up her house, freshen up a bit and start dinner. She is so excited. She hadn't had a date in so long. A date? This isn't date, she thought. This is just a man who invited himself over for dinner. She started questioning why she agreed to this. She must be really desperate. She had just gotten out of a relationship and promised herself she wouldn't get involved with anyone for some time. Desperate or not, it was too late now and she needed to get ready. *Taliah made a big mistake. Women let me tell you something. Please don't allow strangers to come over to your house. Taliah appears to be pretty desperate doesn't she?*

Mr. Foley knocked on the door about two hours later. Taliah was just finishing up the dinner, her house was clean, the food smelled good, and she looked very nice in her red dress. There was a knock on the door again. "Okay, okay; I'm coming." Taliah opens the door.

"Hello Mr. Foley. Good to see you!"

"Wow! Is this the same little lady I met at the store? You are even more beautiful! May I come in?"

"Oh sure, I'm sorry, please come in. Dinner is just about ready."

"What a lovely home you have and something is smelling mighty good. What's on the menu?" "Well, let's see: steamed vegetables, roasted carrots, potatoes and salmon. Go ahead and make yourself at home."

"Thank you." Taliah served dinner for Mr. Foley. They laughed and talked over the meal. They spent hours sharing. They talked about everything and anything including their past relationships and their past failures. Taliah felt so comfortable with Mr. Foley that she opened up and told him everything. He seemed and felt like a father or something. When she was younger, she never really had a relationship with her father. She always wanted one though. Mr. Foley made her feel kind of like a daughter or something, but still like a woman. She told him everything about her past and her future dreams and her previous husbands and how they mistreated her.

Since Mr. Foley was about fifteen years older then her, she knew he would understand and he had experience, so she didn't hesitate to tell him about everything. I mean she told him everything. He had a lot of wisdom and experience with women, and there was something about him that she just absolutely admired. She had to catch herself fast so she wouldn't fall. As she watched him she realized it was too late, she already had fallen and couldn't get up. *Taliah, what are you doing?*

This is a good place to take a note. Ladies, do not pour your soul out to a man you just met. You don't really know him. It doesn't matter how comfortable you think he makes you feel, it's always that way on a first date. Don't tell him everything, keep him in suspense.

Six months later, after the romantic evenings, after the walks in the park holding hands, after the laughing and playing, after the sharing, after the candle light dinners, after the caressing, touching and embracing, and eventually after the many endless nights of love making before marriage, *(Taliah you ought to be ashamed of yourself)*, Mr. Foley proposes to Taliah and they get married. Taliah is on cloud nine on her honeymoon. She thinks finally she has a man that loves her for her. He is everything a girl could ever want. He is rich, good looking, charming, romantic, and the list goes on. This man is too good to be true. But one evening, eight months later, everything changes. Her dreams are shattered. Rob comes home a totally different person. "Taliah, get in here."

"Hi honey. Is something wrong?" Before she can say anything, she finds herself on the floor, her head throbbing in excruciating pain from the blow of the fist by her wonderful Mr. Foley.

"How long did you think you were gonna hide this from me? Huh?"

Taliah was crying and in pain. "Rob, what are you talking about? What's gotten into you? What are you doing? I have never seen you this way. Why did you hit me?"

"Shut up before I hit you again."

"But Rob, I don't know what you are talking about. Please explain to me what's going on."

"You want to know what's going on?" He grabs her roughly by the arm. "Come 'ere, I will tell you what's going on! You are a . . . I can't even say it. How could you do me like this?" Taliah is scared and nervous now. She's not even sure if she should say anything.

"How could you Taliah? I . . . I thought you loved me."

"Rob, you know I love you. What are you talking about? Please, just tell me what you are talking about?"

"I saw you today Taliah."

"You saw me where?"

"I saw you talking and laughing with your lover."

"My lover? What on earth are you talking about, Rob?"

"Don't play Miss Innocent now! I saw you with him. How could you be unfaithful to me? Haven't I been good to you so far? I have been trying really hard to please you and to make you happy. Now you brought out the bad side of me that I didn't ever want you to see. The thought of you being with another man has done something to me. Taliah, tell me what I saw today wasn't true. Tell me?"

"First of all, I'm a little confused because I don't understand how you could have seen me today when you were at work?"

"I didn't go to work today. I took the day off because I wanted to make sure that what I suspected wasn't true. I just knew you were seeing somebody else."

"Now why on earth would you think that? I'm in love with you?"

"Well who was that man that you were with at the store?"

"How did you know I went to the store?"

"I followed you."

"You what? You don't trust me or something? Why are you following me? Have I given you a reason not to trust me?"

"Well . . . I uh . . ."

"Rob, the man I was talking to was an old cousin of mine that I haven't seen in a while and I gave him a hug. I was glad to see him?"

"Your cousin, huh?"

"Yes, my cousin." He pauses and then says to her, "Taliah, come here baby." He holds her in his arms. "I'm so sorry. I didn't mean to hit you. Please don't leave me. You're gonna leave me now aren't you? Please don't leave me. The thought of being without you scares me. I would kill myself if you left me. You are the best thing that has ever happened to me. Please forgive me? I am so sorry. I promise I will never hit you again."

Taliah doesn't say anything, she just starts to cry.

"Taliah? Taliah? I said I was sorry. Stop crying and come 'ere." He pulls her close to him and kisses her passionately. Taliah kisses him back and says, "Why did you hit me. I'm your wife and I'm a lady. You're not supposed to hit women." *Taliah had a flash back to what happened to her when the men slapped her while raping her.* Please don't ever hit me again. That would not be good. You can never hit me again. Do you understand me, Rob? You can never hit me again. I can't be with a man that is violent. I have been through too much. All I want is to be loved, appreciated and respected. So please promise me you won't hit me again? Please promise me?"

"I promise, baby, I promise." They end the night in each other's arms, making love.

Two months later, Taliah was being seen by a doctor regularly because her ex-husband failed to keep all his promises. He beat her up badly. He beat her almost every night and kept making up with flowers, candy, gifts and apologies. Taliah kept taking him back because she thought she could change him. She thought if she loved him hard enough, and was just nice to him, he would change. She started feeling she was causing him to act like this. Besides, he promised to get counseling, and he did go . . . once. But that wasn't it. He even said he would start going to church and he did. But he never changed.

Women, let me tell you something: these abusive men will never change unless they get severe help. Some of these abusive men kill, and you don't want to be with a man that puts you in a position where your life is threatened.

One night, after the last beating almost killed her, Taliah couldn't take it anymore. She left him and never came back. He would follow her, stalk her, and even threatened to kill her.

He eventually gave up and a few months later she received a certificate of divorce in the mail. She was glad about this one. That night, Taliah decided she was through with men. She was through with their rejection, beatings, and their lying and cheating. She couldn't take it anymore. She wondered if there were any good men out there. She doubted it, so this was the last time that she would marry another man. This was her fifth husband, and she still couldn't marry the right one. There was too much heartache and too much pain. From now on, she would break their hearts before they break hers.

So Taliah hid her pain behind a broken smile. She built up hard walls around her heart. She became cold as ice. She stopped wearing perfume, stopped combing her hair, and stopped putting on jewelry. Why should she get all dressed up to attract another man that would just break her heart or beat her? She couldn't take it anymore.

First of all, Taliah, you shouldn't be getting all prettied up to attract men. You should do that for yourself, to feel good about yourself and to keep yourself looking nice. Taliah cries herself to sleep in her room night after night. Depression and darkness becomes her best friend. She had never been a drinker before, but she finds herself turning to alcohol to numb the pain, and then to drugs to make her feel happy. She felt she was dying inside. She even started eating all kinds of foods to ease her emotional uproar, so she gained weight.

Poor Taliah. She doesn't realize that God is the one she really needs to turn to. He is the only one that can mend her broken heart, heal her wounds, quench her thirst and fill the hole within her soul that she so desperately needs filling. God has manifested in the flesh in the form of Jesus waiting at the well. He's waiting to give her a gift, the living water that will not only heal her from all of the past bad relationships, but heal her physically, emotionally and spiritually. He will satisfy her totally. Men always disappointed her, but Jesus would never disappoint her. However, she doesn't know that . . . yet.

Chapter Nine

The Sixth Man
The Live-In Boyfriend

John 4:18
". . . and the one whom you now have is not your husband, in that you spoke truly."

Four months later, after gaining about fifty pounds, Taliah looked in the mirror at herself and didn't like what she saw. What happened to her beautiful curvy shape that men were so attracted to? She no longer had her small waist, or round hips, or plump breasts. All she had was blubber – round, fat blubber. But she didn't care; she knew now that men wouldn't notice her. She was fat, and didn't care how she looked.

However, one day, as she was out in her yard planting, a man came up to her and said, "Uh, excuse me, ma'am."

"Yes, what is it?"

"I just wanted to say how lovely you look out here in the yard planting your garden. I wish I had someone to help me with my garden. Do you think you can help me? I only live a few blocks down the road."

"I'm busy, so no, I don't think so."

"Why not? Please ma'am? I really need your help."

"I said I'm busy, just leave me be."

"Since you are my neighbor, I knew you didn't mean it."

"Yes I did. Now I am very busy and have a lot of work to do. I'm sorry Mister, but the answer is no. I don't have the time, so just leave me alone."

"Okay, tell you what, I will make it really simple for you. Just come over and look at my yard and tell me what I need to do. That's all you have to do. It will only take a few minutes. You have a few minutes to spare don't you?" The man's persistence was getting on Taliah's last nerve. She felt like punching him. She didn't even want to see a man, let alone plant his garden. She didn't know why he was he even talking to her or why she was talking to him. But he kept asking and wouldn't take no for an answer.

"A few minutes huh?"

"Yes ma'am, only a few moments."

"Well OK, but only for a few moments. I don't have time to be doing this; however, I will help you because you are my neighbor, but only for a moment."

"Thank you, ma'am. I'm sorry, what did you say your name was?"

"I didn't say and you don't need to know."

"Boy, somebody must have really hurt you. Why do you seem so angry and bitter and why are you acting so cold?"

"Excuse me?" Taliah said.

"Oh nothing; never mind me. It's none of my business. I didn't mean to pry. Sorry."

She walked to his house with him and he just talked and talked. But Taliah didn't say a word. She really wasn't even listening to him. All she could think about was getting this over with. But when she came to his home, she saw what a beautiful home he had and thought she would love to live in a house like this. She didn't like that little old broken down house she was renting at all, but since she left her last husband, she had to find somewhere to live, quickly, and the little old broken down house with bugs and rats was available.

When she got to her neighbor's house the man said, "This is it. This is where I live. Now I just need a woman's touch and a woman to call this place home."

"Excuse me sir, I really am not interested in your house. Where is the yard?"

"It's right here ma'am," pointing to the front. "Yes ma'am, right here. But I will also need help on the sides of the house and in my back yard. Do you have any ideas?"

"Well, what you need to do is . . ." And as she talked about what he needed to plant in his garden, he was looking at her lustfully thinking about how much he needed a woman, and how this woman had it going on. She has a lot of meat on her bones and I like big women. She reminds me of my momma. I'm sure she can cook like momma and take care of my home like momma did too. I got to get her. I need a woman. I know she's a challenge, but I am not letting this one go. "Okay ma'am. When can we get started?"

"We? There is no we. When can YOU get started? You said it would only take a few moments and I am telling you what you need to do."

"I heard you, but I need to know where to get the seeds and how to plant them. You have to go with me to get the seeds because I am not sure which ones to get. And if you don't mind me asking again, what is your name? Okay, how about if I tell you my name. My name is George."

"So."

"So?"

"Yes so. I don't really care what your name is Mr."

"Now ma'am, you seemed like a nice lady. There's no need to be rude. Please, tell me your name." Taliah hesitates and thinks well he's right, no need to be rude. "Okay, I will tell you my name. My name is Taliah?"

"Taliah huh?"

"Yes Taliah, and that's all you need to know."

"Well that's a lovely name. It matches you. You are very lovely — beautiful even." Taliah thought to herself, *no he didn't tell me I am beautiful as ugly and fat as I look right now.*

"Thank you, but please don't pay me any compliments."

"Yes ma'am; whatever you say. So when can we get started."

"I really don't have the time, but I will help you get started."

"Okay; good enough. How about tomorrow morning?"

"No, I'll be busy tomorrow. How about the next day?"

"Uh, well okay; that will be fine." George said.

"Okay, Mr. George. I gotta go; your minutes are up."

"Thank you so much, Taliah."

"Yeah, yeah. Whatever. No problem."

Six months, later, Taliah moved in with George because of his persistency, his compliments, the desire in his eyes, his charm and charisma, and the way he accepted her even though she was fat. Taliah thought he seemed so different than the rest of them. She said she would not be with another man and she meant it. But what she really meant was that she wouldn't marry another man for them to divorce her whenever they got tired of her. "This time I will leave when I get good and ready." But actually, Taliah thought, she didn't want to leave. This man was special. And he acted like he really loved her. When he made love to her, he took her to another world. The way he touched her and talked gently to her was making her fall madly in love with him.

Taliah, No! Why do you fall so easily in love with these men? You said the same about all of them. And why do you keep giving them your body so easily. Couldn't he just be a friend? You must be desperate for love. But she didn't want him to know that. She would never tell him that she loved him. Although she would love to be his wife, he never asked her to marry him. Deep in her soul, Taliah knew that living with a man was wrong, and having sex outside of marriage was wrong, but she didn't care.

Three months later, things began to change. She wasn't sure about George anymore. There were times when they didn't discuss marriage. Taliah was willing to give marriage another shot one last time, but George didn't seem interested in marrying her. He had been promising to marry her but hadn't proposed yet. As a matter of fact, lately he hadn't shown any interest and didn't seem to desire her anymore.

Taliah, get a hint. He's using you and will never marry you because you gave up your sweet treasures. Why are you living with him in sin anyway? Ladies, remember this: keep your treasure hidden until marriage. Don't try to feed the longings and the emptiness within your soul by turning to sex. Sex won't quench your thirst or fulfill your emotional needs and desires. Neither will a man laying next to you every night just to keep you from being alone.

Women often give their bodies to men so they can be emotionally satisfied. It's not so much the burning in the flesh and the passion they crave, though that occurs too. It's the intense desire and need to feel wanted and desired and emotionally satisfied. However, when a woman gives her body outside of marriage, why would he propose to her? He got what he wanted. Men like challenges, and the challenge was over. There's no need to pursue marriage. This leaves a lot of women heart broken, misused and abused. This is not the plan of God. But realize that you don't have to give a man sex for him to love and desire you. Sex was created to be beautiful; but only within marriage, not outside of marriage. I strongly believe that's why there are so many hurt young teenage girls and women. They give up their bodies expecting to get love in return only to be rejected and misused.

In reality, the men are usually only interested in that one thing, *sex.* They want a challenge. They want to see if they got game and could get the chance to get you in the sack. And of course, women, these are usually the unsaved and ungodly men. *I have counseled and ministered to many women, I have five brothers. Please trust what I say. Most saved Godly men will respect you as you respect yourselves.*

This would be a good place to give you another note. I said *most* saved men, as there are a few in the body of Christ that could be this way. Pray for spiritual discernment, so you will be able to discern when God sends you one of his good boys and not a *wolf in sheep's clothing*. Notice I said, *send* you. *A man that finds a wife finds a good thing and obtains favor from the Lord.* So single women, you don't have to go looking for anybody; he will find you when the season is right — your season and his season. I feel compelled to tell a single woman who is reading this book (and you didn't just pick it up just by accident), if you are doing all the right things: walking with the Lord, coming to church, paying your tithes, using your gifts in the ministry of God, and serving those in need, you are wondering when God will send you a man.

It seems like all your friends, and even younger women, are getting married before you. You wonder when it will be your turn. I have great news for you. The answer is soon. Just wait and pray; then wait and pray some more. God has someone for you. During the waiting period, He is preparing you as well as your mate. When God's time come (catch that: God's timing, not yours) then you two will meet. Wait patiently, humble yourself and dedicate your mind, soul and body to the Lord. Get busy in the ministry serving others and while you are serving, like Ruth, God will send you a Boaz.

What some women fail to realize and understand is when a woman saves herself for marriage, meaning her body, that becomes attractive to a man and makes him desire her more. You don't have to give your body to keep a man. If that is all he wants from you and he is not concerned with your dreams, goals, interests, intellect, spirituality, concerns, etc., then you have the wrong one. Women are disappointed when their lovers are nowhere to be found. Not only did the men get what they wanted and left and never returned calls, but some of them had diseases and passed it on to you and didn't tell you. Remember, there is a consequence to sin.

I believe the fact that people are having sex so freely is why there are so many STD's out there. God has allowed this plague of diseases to creep in because of the uncleanliness and filthiness of sin in the world today. When you have sex outside of marriage, you are committing a sin and you are a fornicator. Sorry to be so blunt but, *the truth will make you free* and I have got to tell the truth to my sisters. Committing sins so freely is not pleasing to God and you are fulfilling the lusts of your flesh. Now, before you feel bad about this, because the majority of women nowadays have had sex outside of marriage. However, once you become a Christian, which means Christ-like, you must refrain from this pleasure. If for some reason you were weak and slipped, ask God to forgive you and cleanse you and He will do just that.

He said in his word, *"If you confess your sins, he is faithful and just to forgive you of your sins."* Just don't remain in sin. *Should you continue in sin that grace should abound? God forbid.* God can help you control the flesh if you ask the Holy Spirit. The burning in your flesh will pass as you steal away in the presence of God daily by meditating on His Word and praying. His presence is so real. His presence is more satisfying than any man. When you do this, you are feeding your spirit, and the Bible says if you *walk in the spirit, you will not fulfill the lusts of the flesh.* The lust of the flesh is anything that gratifies your fleshly desires, including food.

Sometimes women turn to food when they feel lonely, depressed and emotionally unsatisfied. *Taliah did.* They eat and eat all kinds of processed foods that are not good for them and gain unwanted pounds. Then they are more depressed because now they are over weight. Just to give you a tip, if you want to lose weight, drink plenty of water — at least eight glasses a day. Eat fruits and veggies, eat small portions at meal times, and drink herbal teas. Walk at least twenty-five minutes, or longer, a day or do some kind of aerobic or cardio exercise. This is good for you and not just to lose weight, though you will, but to feel great. You should develop this habit and make it a hard habit to break. Make it a life style habit. Take care of yourself girl, because you are not getting any younger. If you think about how it started in the beginning, in the Garden of Eden, the foods that surrounded Adam and Eve were fruits and vegetables. I can just imagine God saying, "Eat the food I originally created for you, not the processed foods. This was my original plan."

I think this is why a lot of women and men for that matter, are developing cancers, diabetes, high blood pressure and dying of heart attacks: they are eating all the wrong foods. If you really knew what was in the bad foods you ate, such as parasites and so on, you would think again before you ate it. Anyway, when the more you feed your spirit the word of God, and the more you pray, you are crucifying the flesh. Do you ever notice when you fast that your body is weak and feels like you are dying? But even though your flesh feels this way, your spirit is revived and strengthened, because you are praying and meditating on the Word of God, which is feeding your soul and your spirit spiritual food. Okay, back to Taliah.

Taliah thought this current relationship wasn't going to work either because of fear, doubt, disappointments and rejections from the past which had lowered her self-esteem, deleted her confidence and replaced it with insecurities. It doesn't matter though, because she feels that she has to have a man to love her. Even if it meant running after her lover, giving up her sweet treasure, losing the respect for herself and her body, she was desperate for love, desperate for attention and desperate to be desired. What Taliah can't comprehend is that she thinks she needs a man to fulfill her but a man can never fulfill her even if she finally finds the right one. Only God can fulfill her every desire, the longing that is so deep within her soul. He left the void there when he created the woman so only He could fulfill it. The emptiness will remain until you allow God to fill it. Taliah thinks she needs the love of a man, and yes it feels good to have a man to love, cherish and respect you. However, no man can ever love you like God can. *For God so loved the world he gave his only begotten son, that whosoever believeth in him should not perish, but have everlasting life.*

Taliah needs to be persuaded that despite the faults she may have, Gods' love covers the multitudes of her faults so that *neither death, nor life, nor angels nor principalities, nor powers, nor height, nor depth nor any other creature shall be able to separate her from the love of God which is in Christ Jesus.* Taliah doesn't realize this, so she is living with this man in sin. While living in this sin, (and you know living with a man without being married is not the will of God) anything is liable to happen in this relationship. Furthermore, she hadn't allowed herself time to heal from the previous relationship. As women, we must allow time for healing after a relationship ends. Use this time to focus on you.

What is your passion? What do you like to do? What do you enjoy doing? Use this time alone to perfect your character. Pamper and beautify yourself. If you feel like crying during the healing process, cry and pray to God and release it at the altar. Depend on Jesus for your total healing. Allow Him to be your husband. Let him lavish His love upon you. His Love is unconditional. He can love you like no man can ever love you, for He is the lover of your soul. God is Love. A man has his own issues to deal with, and he is just but a man. He is not capable of fulfilling your every desire, so lose the expectations. God loves you and He will supply your every need and fulfill your desires if you invite Him in and express your need for Him.

Sometimes God will allow you to get hurt so you will turn to him. *I feel as though I am ministering to some woman right now.* God is a jealous God and He will have no other god (or man) before him. He will allow you to run after your lovers and they will no longer desire you. God says in Hosea 2:7, *and she shall follow after her lovers, but she shall not overtake them, and she shall seek them but shall not find them.* Then in verse 14 he says, *behold I will allure her and bring her into the wilderness and speak comfortably to her.* Well, will you look at that? Our God, our father is so into us, that He allures you into the wilderness so He can speak tenderly, sweetly, and comfortably to you.

I talked about this in my previous chapter. He knows exactly what to say and how to say it. Men, if you are reading this book, take notes. Women love to be spoken to gently and tenderly; not harsh, cold, or cruel. You want to learn how to love a woman? Read the Bible, especially the book of Song of Solomon. Study the scriptures on loving your wife as Christ loved the church. Women, we serve an awesome God that cares about our deepest desires and needs. Stop turning to men to give you the attention and affection you think you need in order to get over the hurt from a previous relationship. All you are doing is putting a band-aid on an open wound that will never heal unless you allow God to heal you. *Render your affection above and not beneath.* Okay, for real, back to Taliah.

Taliah knows that George, her live in man, will probably leave her too. She really didn't know what she saw in George. He was not that good looking and he was boring, dull and nerdy, but he was, somewhat nice to her, compared to the other men she had been with. There was nothing to him, however, she just knew he would be the one she could depend on for her happiness. He would be the one to rescue her from all the hurt and pain. He would love her and hold her and tell her how much he desired her. Her family, and what little friends she had, turned their backs on her. She hoped George wouldn't leave her too, even though now she is sensing that his desire for her is changing because of all the rejection she experienced from her previous men caused her to become very insecure and to doubt their relationship. Maybe this will be the man of her dreams. Maybe he will rescue her. Maybe he will be the one to make me happy. Maybe, maybe, maybe; she sounds like a broken record. She thought surely he'd be waiting for her when she got back home from this desert.

What Taliah doesn't realize is that she can't depend on a man to make her happy. She needs to concentrate on becoming whole by not depending on men to make her happy, but depending on God. She becomes whole only when she surrenders everything to God and allows Him to fill the void of emptiness that is so deep inside her soul. Sad to say, but a lot of women don't think their life is complete unless they have a man. They end up married to a man they just met after coming out of a recent relationship, not allowing themselves time to heal. Can you relate? Are you one of those women? Taliah is included in this bunch because she had been in several relationships. Women, your life becomes complete when you meet Jesus. And guess what? He is waiting and beckoning for you to come to him now. You are not just reading this book by accident. He is waiting for you and has been waiting for you for some time now . . . at the well. Like He is waiting for Taliah at the well, He is also waiting for you my dear sister. Beloved, please don't keep the master waiting.

Chapter Ten

Lost In The Desert

John 17:12
"Not one of them is lost . . ."

Taliah got lost in the desert while searching for love in all the wrong faces. She went through five different types of men, still to remain unsatisfied and unhappy. How many men have you been with and depended on for happiness, only to leave you, unhappy, dissatisfied, heart broken, used up, dissatisfied, depressed, suicidal, insecure and hopeless? I'm sure that at least one of Taliah's husbands could relate to someone you have dated or even married. But you see, Taliah was searching for love in all the wrong faces. She never allowed herself time to heal or time to find herself and who she was. She definitely didn't know Jesus, because if she did, she wouldn't have gone through as many men as she did. Jesus said, *I am the way, the truth and the life. If you find me, you will find life.*

Seek ye first the kingdom of God and his righteousness and all of things shall be added unto you. What things? He means everything that you need, including a husband. Your desires, your wants - whatever you need, He will give it to you, as long as it lines up with His Word and His desires and plans for you. If you put him first, He will give you what you need. However, it does say *many are the desires of a man's heart, but the Lord's purpose shall prevail.* So sometimes things that we desire may not be what God has planned and purposed for us. That's why it is imperative that we pray and ask the Holy Spirit to lead us and guide us to make sure that what we are asking for lines up with the Word of God, and that it is His desire for you. Does having a man or a husband line up with His Word? Yes. Throughout the Bible God speaks about marriages, in the Old and New Testament. So it is God's will that we are married. However, there are some who wish not to marry and remain as a eunuch. Jesus describes this in the book of Matthew 19:7-12. Jesus and his disciples were having a discussion regarding marriage, divorce, unfaithfulness, and the reason for divorce due to adultery. One of the disciples makes a statement that perhaps it was better not to marry. But then Jesus states that not all can accept this statement. Only those who God helps. Some become eunuchs, which could mean to refrain from sexual relations or the inability to perform due to the removal of a man's testicles or because they do not function. Then he says that some have been made that way by others, and some choose not to marry for the sake of the kingdom of heaven. So some people prefer not to be married.

Then there are those who would like to be married and it is better to marry then to burn with passion. However, God knows that some wives would put that husband or man before Him, and some women may not yet be ready for marriage. Is your house presentable for a husband, do you keep it clean? Are you preparing yourself to be that good wife? Are you selfish, insecure, unstable, needy, and are you whole. He did say a man who finds a wife finds a good thing. Will you be good for the man that God sends you? However, when God finally sends him, it will be in his own timing not yours. And his timing is always right on time, even though it may seem to be taking a while. If it has been one year or ten years, you must wait on God's best.

But you see, this is a problem for most of us women. We can't wait. We are in such a hurry to get married or have a man we can't wait. We settle for less because of loneliness instead of waiting for God's best. Since we can't wait, we get lost in our desert of desperation, uncertainties, pain, and confusion like Taliah did. People don't like being lost. It is frustrating when you are lost. The definition of lost is to cause to miss one's way or bearings, to make (oneself) withdrawn from immediate reality, to wander, or go astray. Sometimes when you are lost, you become stressed, uncertain of who you are, insecure, irritated, inpatient, and moody. It is as though you are in a maze and you keep going around in circles not knowing how to get out. You may ask the questions: Can't they see I'm struggling and confused out here alone? Don't they know I'm lost? Why won't they help me find my way? Can somebody help me find my way? Is anybody out there that even cares that I'm lost? How did I get out here in the first place? It seems as though I have been lost in this maze for years. No one has even offered to help me find my way. So many questions why, and no one to answer them. And it's only because they haven't asked the one . . . the omniscient one . . . the one who knows everything. Why not ask God? And so, this person remains lost in this maze.

One thing the lost person has to understand is that you are lost because you haven't found Jesus. Jesus said, *"I am the way, the truth and the life."* In order to find your way you must find Jesus because He is the way. He is your way out of every situation. He is your way out of darkness because He is the light. There is no confusion in Him, because God is not the author of confusion. He is the door of light in your maze. *I am the door.* He is the window of light in your tunnel of darkness; He is your every thing. Find Jesus and you will find your way. Find Jesus and you will find truth. Find Jesus and you will find life. If you lose anything, you should lose your life in Christ and when your life is lost and hidden in Christ, you can't find your life unless you find Christ. Get it?

Even though you have strayed and you are lost, Jesus said, *and not one of them are lost* because you were chosen before the foundations of the world. Jesus knew that you would get lost, especially in the desert. So He allures and helps you find your way. Taliah doesn't realize yet that Christ is what she needs, so she remains lost for a while, in this hot desert, wandering helplessly, thinking about her past husbands. Her mind has gone hay wild. Instead of filling it with thoughts of positive things, she fills it up with her past and present lovers.

About half way through her journey, Taliah stopped in the midst of her thinking and looked around. "Where am I?" she wondered. "It looks like I am in the middle of nowhere. Am I lost? Oh I hope not." As she looked further, she noticed there were two roads; one going east and the other going south. Where did these roads come from? Did they just suddenly appear? And where do they lead? *There goes Taliah with all of her questions again.* I know I don't have too much longer. "Oh, if I can just make it to the well. I am so thirsty. If I can just draw some water from the well. Which one of these roads should I take and where do they lead?" *This is the way . . . walk in it.*

What! Who? Who said that? Did I just hear a voice? Now, she knows she has not only lost her way, but now she has lost her mind. Has anyone seen my mind she asked? I have lost it. She's hearing voices again that she doesn't recognize. She thinks she is going crazy. If her third husband could see her now, he would probably think she was crazy. She's out in this hot desert not knowing which way to turn. She started out just wanting to go and draw some water from the well. Now she's lost and confused and roads are appearing from out of nowhere. "What's going on?" She feels so alone and confused. "What's wrong with me?" She thought. "Am I losing it?" What she thought was a short journey, ends up being a long, discouraging one. And actually, her journey ends up being longer than she expected.

While she was on her journey, she complained about everything. She didn't understand why bad things kept happening to her and why she met all the wrong men. "What did I do to deserve this?" she thought. She was lonely, depressed, hungry, and needed someone to love her for real, for real. She couldn't help to complain because there was nothing to be grateful for, or so she thought.

This is a good place to take a note. While you are on your journey, do not murmur and complain. You have so much to be grateful and thankful for. When the children of Israel murmured and complained it did not get them to the promise land now did it? God sent snakes to kill them because of their murmuring and complaining. I know that seems a bit harsh and extreme, but God does not like it when his children complain - especially His chosen ones, the called out ones. He's referring to the ones He delivered and kept delivering with His miraculous wonders and the ones He freed from bondage. But these, his children, still complained after God delivered them from Pharaoh's slavery and bondage in Egypt. They complained about being better off in Egypt, with good food to eat because they felt they were starving to death in the wilderness. But when they got hungry, God fed them by raining down manna or angels food from heaven.

What father wouldn't feed their children if they were hungry? They ate but then became ungrateful and got tired of eating the same food. They wanted some meat, so God gave them quails to eat. Or should I say in modern terms, chicken to eat. Then they complained about not having water because they were thirsty. So God gave them sweet water to drink from the rock. See, God will take care of you on your journey, even in spite of your ugliness, meanness, nasty attitude, emotions, and menopause. He still loves you and will take care of you while you are lost in your maze, while you are confused, when you are hurting, hungry and thirsty. God will take care of you. God's grace and mercy covers us and we are not even worthy of His grace. His grace is sufficient for thee.

I know there are times we don't know which way to go, or which road to take. We all want to make the right choices and take the right road that will lead to our destiny . . . our future . . . at least down the right path. However, we do get lost along the way, which causes discouragement. In order to find our way, however, we must turn to the master, Jesus. I said it before so I will say it again, Jesus said, *this is the way walk ye there in it. I am the way, the truth and the light.* Jesus said *if I lost one sheep out of ninety-nine, I would go after that one to find it.* God cares that much about you. Beloved, give your life to Jesus and His Holy Spirit will lead the way and help you find your way when you are lost. He will lead you, guide you, comfort you and rebuke you. What Taliah should have done, was ask help from the Holy Spirit, which is the living water. However, Taliah hasn't met the living water yet so she has no idea. She doesn't know that Jesus will lead her and guide her and even hold her hand along the way. He will never let her go because He said that He would *never leave you nor forsake you.* Jesus is passionately in love with you and can't wait to meet you at the well. And He feels the same way about all of his daughters and sons.

However, Taliah's mind, heart and soul are not ready to receive Him. She is lost and confused and all her mind can think about is finding her way to the well that suddenly seems so far away. Her throat is dry, her lips are chapped, and her body is drenched from sweating because of walking in this hot desert. Her feet are sore and throbbing from walking so long. She is desperate to quench her dying thirst with a drink from the well. As she is standing there still deciding which road to take, she hears the same voice again saying, *this is the way; walk in it.* Who keeps saying that? She is frightened by the voice and begins to run. As she is running, she doesn't know if she is heading east or south. Well, it doesn't matter now. She will get to the well.

She stops running because she is now out of breath. She looks down at her sandals and notices she has a hole that decided to create itself on the bottom of her shoe. "Oh no! Now I am going to get a blister. What is going on?" Certainly there is more to life than traveling down this long, dreary road with a hole in my worn out shoes. I have no idea why I am here in the first place. I don't even know where I belong. All of my husbands rejected me, and I'm starting to think the man I'm living with now doesn't want me anymore. The people of the town stare and look at me funny, like I am dirty or something. My family has turned their back on me. I have no one. I mean no one that will be there for me for real. Now I am lost in this God-forsaken desert. God, where are you? Hey, if you are up there, can you hear me? Why do you have me out here in this hot never-ending desert? Not only am I in this desert, now I'm lost in it. If you cared anything about me, you would help me find my way. Taliah caught herself. "Wait a minute, am I talking to God again? I think they call this praying. Well, I'm not praying. I just have a lot of questions but no one to answer them. And, well, God is available and although I know he's not really listening to me. I have a lot of sin in my life, and sin separates me from God." *Taliah God does hear you and He is drawing you.* Taliah sat down and put her head in her lap and cried herself to sleep in the hot desert, where there was no water visible, no food, nobody but her. She remained lost in the desert, but only for a while because someone is waiting and drawing her nearer to him. She just doesn't realize who He is yet.

Chapter Eleven

Climbing Up The Mountain
Faith

Hebrews 11:1
"Now faith is the substance of things hoped for and the evidence of things not seen."

Taliah woke up after taking a nap. She stood up to start her journey again to find the well. She lifted up her head and looked up, the sun was beaming in her face, the raves from the heat of the sun were so hot, she felt like she was about to pass out. As she looked up, she saw a mountain right in the middle of the desert. She didn't remember seeing this mountain before. Where had it come from? It just popped up from nowhere. She wondered what was up there. Could she make it up the mountain? It wouldn't hurt to try. She began walking towards the mountain and decided that it was too big for her to climb. She just ignored it and kept walking. But the more she ignored it, the more the mountain appeared to get bigger and bigger.

She was curious, and thought maybe she could climb it. As she was climbing the mountain, but she didn't realize how big it was. She thought she could climb the mountain, then she began to doubt herself and wanted to get down. But something in her was determined to get to the top of the mountain. And besides, how could she get to the well with this big mountain in the way? So she kept climbing. As she was climbing, she slipped and almost lost her grip, but determination kept her going. Finally she reached the top. She made it! She smiled and forgot all about her problems because she made it to the top. She looked up into the sky, exhaled and thought about how beautiful and peaceful it was up here. She'd never noticed how beautiful God's creation was. The clouds formed so perfectly, the birds flying and chasing one another with no cares. Finally, she could breathe fresh air. The light from the sun began to shine brighter; so bright in her eyes that she couldn't see. She tried to turn around but couldn't see. She slipped and fell and she couldn't get a grip.

So she fell, helpless and hopeless, from the top of the mountain. As she was falling, she prayed for God to save her. She fell to the ground and was knocked unconscious. As she was out, she thought she heard a voice in her conscience calling her name. *"Taliah, Taliah."* She came to herself slowly and brushed the dirt off her dress. She had a few bruises but that was all. *"Taliah, Taliah"* a still small voice said again. She was startled and said, "Who's there?" There was nothing but silence. Maybe she was hearing voices again. She got up and continued on with her journey, forgetting about the mountain and started walking towards the well again. She was so thirsty. If she could just get past this mountain to get to the well, she could get a drink and quench her thirst.

Ladies, as you are on your journey, you may experience a mountain along the way. Don't give up. God will give you the strength to climb the mountain. If you fall, please get back up. He may even move the mountain out of the way. But in most cases, He won't. He gives you the mountain so that you can depend on Him to give you the strength to climb it. As a songwriter once said, Lord don't move the mountain, just give me the strength to climb it. Can you imagine yourself on the top of your mountain? Because on the top of the mountain you are above your problems, above every situation that tries to keep you down. Taliah was curious about the mountain because it appeared out of nowhere. She was already in a desert and now this mountain appeared. Like Taliah, I'm sure you have encountered many mountains that appeared out of nowhere along your journey in life. An unexpected mountain, a blow, a daughter that you just found out was pregnant, a son on drugs, a husband that you discovered was cheating, a bad report from the doctor, or you may have just lost a loved one. Whatever your mountain was, how did you handle it? Did you have the courage to climb it or did you suppress your feelings and went around the mountain or ignored it? If you went around it, guess what? The mountain will still be there.

I believe that as children of God we need to climb the mountains, accept the mountains, deal with the mountains and pray about the mountains. Ask God to help you with this mountain. By the way, He is the one that allowed it to happen because he is sovereign and He holds all power in his hands. While climbing the mountain we may get weak and tired, but God will give you the strength to climb it. You may fall down like Taliah did, but if you are a child of God you can fall down seven times and because of His sufficient grace and His tender mercies, you can keep getting back up. Please don't stay there because of guilt and condemnation, just keep getting back up and one of these days, you will get it right. Never give up, never get tired, and don't get frustrated. You can make it because *you can do all things through Jesus Christ who strengthens you.*

Another area you must realize is when your mountain comes, and it will, you must have faith and trust that God will give you the strength to climb it. As Jesus approached the fig tree for fruit, He realized that there was no fruit on it, so He cursed it. His disciples were amazed. But Jesus, said, *"If you have faith as small as a grain of a mustard seed you can say unto this mountain be thou removed and be cast into the sea and it shall be given unto you."* You can develop a faith that will move mountains as you trust and depend on God while you travel along your journey. You need faith in order to make it to the top of the mountain. In this life you will not be able to escape the mountains that you face, or the trials and the tests so you might as well hold on, believing that this too shall pass and that you are going to make it. The road that God has placed you on may not be easy, but he wouldn't have brought you this far to leave you. Besides, the trials or tests that come your way are designed to make you stronger. You may not be able to see it during the fiery trial, but believe me, it will make you stronger. You may wonder how it happened and why it happened to you. But as long as you are a believer and follower of Jesus Christ, you will partake in His sufferings.

So don't think it's strange that this strange thing has happened to you. Have joy. Yes, that's right, joy. I know it's hard to have joy and be happy when you are suffering, but why choose to be sad, depressed, mean, and irritated, when you can choose life and be happy, joyful, and at peace and able to rejoice despite your sufferings? In I Peter 4:12 it says *Beloved, think it not strange concerning the fiery trial which is to try you, as though some strange thing happened to you, but rejoice, inasmuch as ye are partakers of Christ's sufferings, that, when his glory shall be revealed ye may be glad also with exceeding joy.*

You also may not know how you are going to make it through this tough time, because you really can't see a way out. But faith will find a way. As long as you trust God, believe and have faith, you will make it up your mountain. Hebrews 11:1 says, *Now faith is the substance of things hoped for and the evidence of things not seen.* If you believe that you can make it you will. Have faith and trust God. Besides, this world belongs to God. He created it. He is that Jehovah Elohim, the God who created the universe. He created you. So since He created you, you should have enough faith to trust Him to take care of His own creation right? Yes, even as you are climbing your mountain, even as you go through the storms, even when you experience the unexpected, have faith and trust that God is on your side and He will get you through this. I promise you He will if you turn to Him. Nothing is too hard or impossible for God. You can't do anything without Him. The reason why things never work out for you is because you keep trying to do everything yourself.

I can just imagine seeing God now, shaking His head saying, *"If my daughters would only listen to me, just trust me, have faith and believe in me I will get her through this. Don't they realize who I am? I am more then any man could ever be."* But Taliah didn't know that. She made all the wrong choices. Now she was lost in the desert, experiencing mountains that she couldn't climb, and thinking about men that broke her heart. If she would have made better choices in life, she would not be in the situation she is in now — hurting, confused, lonely and desperate to experience true love. If women of today can make better choices in life, by checking with the one who made the world before making decisions, and read His book, the *Bible,* they would save themselves a lot of heartache.

So Taliah continues on her journey, after climbing her mountain and then falling, she dare not try to climb it again. She stands up to start her journey again towards the well only to see the two roads again, heading east and south. Not again. She didn't know which way to go? When you don't know what to do and which way to go, stand still and know that He is God. His Spirit will lead the way . . . if you trust Him.

Chapter Twelve

Stand
Still

Exodus 14:13
"Stand still . . . and see the salvation of the Lord."

I can only imagine what was going on in this woman's mind, Taliah, now that she discovered she was lost in the desert. She was confused, uncertain, fearful, doubtful, hopeless, faithless, dehydrated, lonely, and depressed. She wanted to turn back and forget about this whole thing, but would probably get lost heading back. All of these thoughts bombarded her mind. Even though there was a thought mind invasion, Taliah needed to realize where the thoughts were coming from and how severe these thoughts were. This is a good place to take a note. Women you have to realize that you cannot allow your mind to get the best of you. Don't lose your mind to negative thoughts one after another. Your negative thought is like a fiery dart. If one starts, there are several more to come.

Do you realize that bad things happen because it started in the mind? When you dwell on these negative thoughts, they begin to settle and you accept them. Joyce Meyer has a book entitled, The Battlefield of The Mind and Bishop Noel Jones also has a book out similar to this title. That's why it is so important that you do not dwell on these kinds of thoughts because they are of the devil. II Corinthians 10:5 says, *"Cast down every imagination, and every high thing that exalteth itself against the knowledge of God, and bringing into captivity every thought to the obedience of Christ.* "So any negative thought that tries to take over your mind, know that it is not of God, but is an attack from the enemy. So you must cast it down. Replace that thought with good thoughts. Think of good things. *Think on whatsoever things are lovely, whatsoever things are pure, whatsoever things are of good report, think on these things.* Keep your mind on Jesus. He said *He who keeps his mind on me, I will keep him in perfect peace.* So keep your mind on Jesus. He has done so much for you, how can you not think about Him?

Because you are human and in survival mode, you are liable to experience all kinds of negative thoughts when you are trying to survive. Simply because of the spiritual warfare in the flesh and in the mind, we will discuss this in another chapter. But if you dwell on these thoughts, you will remain unfocused and confused, not knowing which way to go. And fear will overtake you if you let it. Please know that *God has not given you the spirit of fear but power and of love and of a sound mind.* Taliah was losing hope because she had been through so much with men and now she is lost in a desert, thirsty, lonely and confused, not knowing which way to go. Taliah wondered how she ended up there. How and when did she begin making all the wrong choices? Well, she doesn't know whether she should go east, west, north or south. Maybe she should just commit suicide because deep depression has smothered her.

Suicidal woman, let me tell you something, please do not harm yourself. It's not worth it. You have a lot to live for. Don't allow depression to get the best of you. Wipe your eyes, don't cry, for there is yet hope. I promise you. There is hope in Jesus Christ. Your savior, your redeemer and deliverer can heal you now. He will give you the joy that you long for, the happiness that you deserve, the peace that passes all understanding, the power that will sustain you, and He will give you a reason to live. And guess what? He is waiting for you at the well.

Taliah was miserable and did not enjoy her life. Something was missing but she just didn't know what and she didn't know how to go about finding what she needed. She thought that men were what she needed, but now she is beginning to realize that they're not. She has had six men and none of them, I mean not even one, could satisfy her needs. She felt empty inside and uncertain of what to do next. When you don't know what to do, stand still. *Stand still and see the salvation of God.* He really cares about what you are going through and is just waiting for you to surrender your life to Him. Sometimes it is best to stand still, pray and wait on God before making decisions - especially when you are in an emotional state. When you make decisions when your emotions are all out of whack, you most often make the wrong decisions.

Taliah was standing there, still not knowing which road to take. She hears a voice that says, *"Stand still."* There is that voice again. This time Taliah replies, "Okay God, if that's you speaking to me and I sense in my spirit that it is, please show me the way. Which one of these roads should I take? I am tired and thirsty and I need some water. Please God, tell me which one of these roads to take. Can you hear me? Please help me God." Taliah starts to cry and walk. While she is crying, she clearly hears a melody in her ear and she begins to sing it:

I'm walking down a lonely road,
Not knowing which way to go,
I've entered in my wilderness,
I know that I am in a test.
In an unfamiliar place,
I'm longing oh to see His face.
Which one of these roads should I take?
Should I run or should I stay?
I can hear him say, "Stand still, still, stand still."
I can hear him say, "Stand still, my child, this is my will."

Taliah falls to her knees and begins to pray. "Oh God. I will stand still I won't run anymore. I know I have done wrong. Please forgive me and show me the way."

Then she hears a voice say, *"This is the way, walk ye in it."* "Okay, I will take this road." Taliah gets up and starts walking down the road that she feels in her spirit God directed her to. As she starts walking down the road, she notices that it is getting dark. What happened to the sunshine so quickly? I have to get to the well before it gets too dark or I won't be able to see my way. Day is almost over and night is just around the corner. Taliah stumbles in the dark.

While traveling on the right road, darkness follows her to try and stop her from seeing her way. She can't see her way that well because of the darkness. She is now hungry because she hasn't eaten anything all day. Of course she is still thirsty because she hasn't gotten to the well yet. Where is the well? All Taliah wanted was some water, she was not trying to go through all of this? Now it's dark and she can't see her way. She is scared and lonely. Where were all those men who were supposed to protect her? She even thought about George back at the house, who hadn't bothered to come looking for her. She has been gone all day and no word from him. And where was God? He led her down this road, only to get blinded by the darkness. "Where are you God? I need you . . . again."

Taliah falls to her knees and cries herself to sleep. She's alone again in the darkness. Depression finds her and smothers her again. Still, she journeys, but on the right road this time.

Chapter Thirteen

In The
Valley Low

Psalm 42:5
    "Why are you so disquieted oh my soul, hope thou in God."

Taliah falls asleep that night on the road in the hot desert. She wakes up and it is morning. "What am I doing out in the middle of the road? Where am I? I know George is worried sick. Or maybe he's not. He doesn't care about me. If he did, he would know that I am lost out in this desert and at least come looking for me. But he didn't. I guess I will continue my journey by myself to the well so I can draw some water. It's time for this journey to be over. I know I had a rough night last night, but I'm okay now; I think. Well, no I'm not. But I will be. I am determined now to find the well. It can't be too much longer, and besides, God told me this is the right road."

Taliah starts walking down the road when, all of sudden, she falls into a valley. "Oh no! Help! Somebody help!" She tries to get out but she can't. She tries to climb up, but her feet are hurting so bad from walking in her old worn out sandals with the hole in it. "I can't believe this is happening to me. It seems like everything is going wrong in my life."

"Well believe it." A woman said.

"Who said that?"

"I did." A woman came out from behind her in dirty clothes and smelling badly. "Hi, my name is Maya."

"Well, hello Maya. My name is Taliah. What are you doing down here and where are we?" "Well, actually, this is where I live."

"You live?"

"Yep; for the past five years."

Another lady comes out; a big lady. "Hi. I'm Lori. I live here too!"

Then another woman comes out. She's a little old thing. "Hi, I am Shamba, and I have been living here longer than all of them."

Taliah was in shock to see all these women. She wasn't sure what to say. Then the little woman continued to say, "I know you are wondering what we are doing down here in this valley low. Well, I'm going to tell you. Come in and have a seat. Taliah wondered where they wanted her to sit because there were no seats.

Taliah followed the little old lady down a dark tunnel to a corner of the valley. Here she had some big rocks with blankets and a few leaves on top of them, I guess to make the rocks comfortable. "I know you are wondering what these are. They're our homemade rocking chairs." Taliah laughed and said, "Okay sure; if you say so. I will try to sit down on your rocking chair." Taliah sat down and thought to herself, *I know they don't think that these rocks are comfortable* . . . then the little old woman said, "I know you think these rocks are not comfortable, but they are very comfortable 'cause this is all we have and we have gotten use to them, so don't be making fun of my chairs. I made them myself. I see a chuckle coming on you."

"Whatever do you mean, I'm not chuckling. But okay, if you say these are chairs, then indeed they are, that's fine by me. Now tell me, why are you all here?"

"Good question, I'm glad you asked. Ladies come over here and sit down with are guest. What did you say your name was?"

"Taliah."

"Okay, Tatayaliah."

"Not Tatayaliah, Taliah."

"Yeah, yeah, whatever; I thought that is what I said. Besides, you got a strange name. Anyway, we are women that have been down in this old valley for a long time. We have cried here, some have prayed here, we have talked about our problems and we have talked about the men in our lives that have rejected us, misused us, abused us, and took advantage of us. All of us were destroyed by men. My husband died, and that's why I'm here. I couldn't go on without him. So I plan to die here in this valley all by my lonesome."

"But why do you want to stay here in this valley?" Taliah asked. "Don't you want to get out of here?"

"Nope. This place here I call home. You see I'm comfortable here."

"How can you be comfortable?" I know I just happened to fall into this valley, and I am not about to get comfortable. I am going to get out. I am not going to stay here. I got a man waiting for me back at home. I just came out here to draw some water from the well."

"Ooooh, I love your attitude." Lori said. "You've got some uummph!" The other women start laughing.

"Well at least you ladies got some joy down here in this valley, but I can't stay here."

"Why don't you tell us about yourself, Ms. Taliah, and tell us about this man you got back home?"

"It's a long story and I don't really have time to tell you because I am tired and this has been a long journey. However, I will just be brief. Right now I am miserable. I am hurting, lonely, confused, depressed, and thirsty. I have tried men after men going from one relationship to another and no one can seem to satisfy me. Now, I am currently living with a man who I feel doesn't love me anymore and who has been promising to marry me. I have been abused, raped, rejected, beat, and the list goes on. And I can't take it anymore. I have been trying to heal my wounds by going from one relationship to another. Yet, I'm still missing something and I don't know what that something is. I haven't allowed myself the time to heal either. I feel something is missing. I don't know yet what it is, but I am determined to find it."

"Lady, you have been through a lot and you still holding on." Maya said.

"I guess I am, but I'm at my breaking point. I can't take this kind of life any more. I am tired of being on this journey that was meant to only be a few hours. All I wanted was to draw some water from the well, and seems I have been on this journey forever and now I am down here in this dirty, stinkin' valley. No offense, but I don't belong here!! You hear me? I don't belong here!"

"Alright, just calm dawn Ms. Lady, calm down. It's going to be alright."

"I am calm! You all can stay down here as long as you want, but I have to get out of here." Taliah starts crying out all of her emotions to these strange women. And they came around her and started crying too.

"Taliah, we don't really want to be here either." Maya says. "At least I don't, but we are stuck." "There is no way out of this valley. I'm sorry to tell you this, Ms. Lady, but you can't get out. There is no way out."

"Oh there is a way out. If there is a way in there is definitely a way out. You ladies just haven't taking the time to find it. But I am going to get out of here. Again, if you all want to stay here, and I know you really don't, then that's on you. But I am getting out of here. I will find a way. God help me, I will find away."

"Did she say God? Please. God doesn't care about us women down in this valley." Lori, the big woman, said. "If He did, He wouldn't leave us here all broken up, misused, abused, and all used up. Let me ask you a question, Ms. Lady, why would God allow us to go through all the hurt and the pain? Why did he give us bad men that broke our hearts and took advantage of us? Is it because we are women? If it wasn't for us having each other to cling too, I don't know where we would be."

"Well, I uh, I really don't have the answers to that, but I know in my heart there is a God. And I think He has been calling and pulling at me or something. I heard His voice and, I don't know, maybe that's why I kept getting hurt by men. And maybe that's why all of us women keep getting hurt because maybe . . . maybe the voice that has been calling us we have been ignoring and the voice wants us to turn to Him first."

One of the other women spoke up, the skinny, middle-aged lady who looked sick. "Taliah, you are right. That voice has been calling us, and I have allowed the voice to help me, unlike some other women I know. But there is indeed a God. You must have faith and trust in Him. That's what I've been doing down in this valley and trying to tell these here other women about Him, who, by the way, just won't listen. Doesn't matter what you going through dear, God is with you because He does love you. I know He loves me, even though I'm weak and sick he still loves me. I have this incurable disease that is killing me. I know I'm dying. But I trust that one day God will heal me. I have faith and I am holding on to it."

"Yeah, yeah, you holding to it alright." Lori said. "You been holding and waiting for a long time and God ain't healed you yet. Where is your God? Like I said, He doesn't care anything about us down here."

"Well I'm so sorry about your illness and I hope you do get well. But like I said, I can't stay down in this valley, I really have to go. It was nice meeting you though and sharing with all of you. I'll be prayin' for . . . I mean . . . uh I uh . . . never mind. I gotta go."

Taliah turns and starts running with determination to find a way out of the valley, but it seems as though she was going around in circles. She thought if there was a way in, there must be a way out. She starts looking for the hole that she fell down in and she notices a light. She had run so far towards the light that she could no longer hear the women's voices in the valley nor see them. She hesitated, stopped and looked back, but she couldn't see anything. She didn't realize how long this valley was? But she couldn't look back; she had to get to the light. She started to climb up towards the light thinking that this has to be the hole that I fell in, but only to discover it was a flashlight left on. A flashlight! I thought this was . . . well, doesn't matter, I will not be discouraged. I am going to find a way out of here. Oh God, please help me get out this valley. Then, out of the blue, she found the hole that she fell into and miraculously, Taliah was able to get out. So she starts her journey again to the well.

Chapter Fourteen

The Lover
of My Soul

John 4:26, 28
*"I that speak to thee . . . am He . . . the woman then left
her waterpot, and went her way into the city, and said to the men,
come, see a man, which told me all things that ever I did: is not
this the Christ?"*

"Finally, I am out of that valley. It's so bright out here. I
can't believe those women down there. I guess they had a point.
Why would God allow us women to go through as much as
we do? Why would he?" As she thought on these things, she
looked down the desert road, and finally saw the well. "Yes!
There's the well. I finally made it. It was hard to get to it but I
finally made it! With her bucket still swinging in her hand, she
starts running to the well with her blistered feet, in her worn
out sandals with the hole in it, and her dirty clothes and messed
up hair. As she runs, she slips and falls and her bucket falls out
of her hand and rolls down by the well. She gets up and dusts
herself off. She goes to pick up her bucket and she notices a
man sitting on the well far off. What! Is that a man? As she gets
closer she notices him watching her. Is that a Jew? What is he
doing over here on our side of town and what is he staring at?
As she picks up her bucket and approaches the well, he says to
her, *"Give me a drink."* Taliah looks around her shoulder and
says to herself, I know he's not asking me for a drink as thirsty
as I am and I haven't even got a drink for myself yet. As long as

I have been walking on this journey and as tired as I am? I just know he didn't . . . *"Give me a drink."* Now he done asked me again. "Look Mr., who you asking for a drink and why are you asking me? Aren't you a Jew? I am a Samaritan woman and Jews have no dealings with Samaritan women, so why are you even talking to me?"

"Woman if you knew the gift of God, and who it is that says to you give me a drink, you could have asked Him and He would have given you living water."

"Look, first of all, I don't care who you are and you don't know me to be asking me to give you some water. You are not even supposed to be talking to me. Besides, the well is deep and you have nothing to draw with. I have my bucket so where's your bucket? If I did decide to give you a drink, how can I do that 'cause you are not drinking out of my bucket. Plus, the well is deep. How are you going to get this living water?" No he didn't ask me for some water, Taliah thought. And then had the nerve to call it, wait a minute. Did he say living water? "Excuse me sir, correct me if I am wrong, but did I just hear you say living water? How is it that your water is living? What, is the water alive or something? Is it breathing?"

"Yes. And I would have given you my living water if you'd asked me."

"Okay, then are you greater then our father Jacob which gave us this well and drank from it himself? As a matter of fact, his children and his cattle drank from this well. That's why I came out here to this well because this is the best well in the desert."

The man at the well answered and said unto her, *"Whoever drinks of this water will thirst again, but whoever drinks of the water that I will give him shall never thirst, because the water that I shall give him shall be in him a well of water, springing up into everlasting life."*

Taliah thought this man must be crazy. What kind of water is he talking about? So she said unto him, "Okay sir give me this water, because if you only knew what it took for me to come out here to draw this water, you would be wondering how in the world I made it. But this water sounds refreshing and since you say it is everlasting, please, I would like to have this water so I won't thirst anymore, neither come out in this long hot desert to draw."

Jesus said to her, *"Okay I will. But first go and get your husband and come back."* No he didn't go there - all up in my business. It sounds like he's trying to get kind of personal. So Taliah said, "Mr., I don't have a husband and don't want another one either." Like it's any of his business, Taliah thought. Why did I even tell him that?

But Jesus said to her, *"Yes, you said it right and said it very well. I have no husband, for you have actually had five husbands and the one who you are living now with is not your husband, as you had said it earlier, you spoke the truth."*

No he didn't! How did he know my business? Taliah starts getting kind of emotional and spiritual and wonders if he's a prophet? How else would he know this unless God told him? So Taliah said, "Sir, I perceive that you are a prophet. Well, since you're a prophet, let me tell you something, our fathers, as I was mentioning earlier, worshiped on this mountain, and you Jews say that Jerusalem is the place where one ought to worship."

Jesus said to her, *"Woman, believe me, the hour is coming when you will neither worship on this mountain, nor in Jerusalem worship the father. You worship what you do not know. We know what we worship, for salvation is of the Jews. But the hour is coming, and now is, when the true worshipers will worship the Father in spirit and truth for the father is seeking such to worship Him in spirit and in truth. God is a Spirit, and those who worship Him must worship Him in spirit and in truth."*

The woman said to Him, "I know that Messiah is coming who is called Christ, when He comes, He will tell us all things." I can just hear Jesus saying to himself, *if this broken woman only knew who I am. That I am God manifested in flesh as Jesus, the Son of God, she would be astonished. She doesn't realize that I am the one who will transform her life. She doesn't realize that I am the one that will make her whole, not all the men she has been with. That's why she is still left unsatisfied because when I created her, I left a void within her soul that only I can fill. No man, nor thing, no flesh, can fill that void. I am the only one that can and will fill and satisfy that void. I am what she has been searching for. I will meet all her needs. Men will never fulfill all of her desires, wants and needs. Only I can. If women would learn to seek me first, my kingdom and my righteousness, refrain from sinning, then I will give them what they need. I will love them so hard - a love that goes beyond this world. A love that is so deep that they can't go under it, so wide that they can't go around it, so high that they can't go above it. A love that is unconditional and everlasting. My love goes beyond human love. It is the agape love; a selfless love. This Samaritan woman will soon realize that.*

So Jesus said to her, *"I who speak to you am He. I am the long awaited Messiah."* This time Taliah didn't ask any more questions. She was stunned. She was shocked. Her emotions were overwhelming inside. All of a sudden it felt like the hole deep in her soul immediately closed up. Suddenly she felt like she had a new heart and it was bursting with joy about ready to explode! She felt all of her heavy burdens lift off of her chest. She felt all the wounds and pains of the past heal instantly and she felt like she was flying high above all of her problems. She no longer thought about the five husbands in her past or her current man for that matter. She found another man. A man that just healed her instantly, and none of those men could ever do that. The feeling that she got didn't even compare to the men that she had been with. She had the bucket still in her hand ready to draw water from the well, but after Jesus said he was the Messiah, she immediately believed, so she dropped her water bucket. She no longer needed the water that she thought she needed. Her thirst was quenched.

Did you catch that? *She dropped her water bucket.* This is almost the most important part. She dropped her water bucket. Have you dropped your water bucket yet? She knew there was something different about this man when she first met him. She thought He was nothing like all the other men. It was like, this man was not from this world, sounds crazy, but it's true. He did appear to look different. There was something about this man. There was a peace and love that was flowing from within him. He can't be of this world. Could he be? Oh goodness, He said he was God in flesh. Oh my! Could it really be Him? And He was talking to me? Me! In my dirty clothes, my messed up hair and my blistered feet. Oh! I've got to go tell the women in the valley. I've got to go. But I want to stay with Him. But I can't. I must tell the others that the Messiah is here!

Jesus smiled because He knew what was going on in her mind. He heard every thought. The men that were with Him were coming back from the city. They had noticed Him talking to her earlier and wondered why He continued this conversation. And now Jesus was smiling. He wasn't supposed to be talking to her. This was against the Jewish law. But they dared not ask him why He was talking to this Samaritan woman.

Taliah was so overwhelmed that she didn't even notice the men approaching. She ran past them and through the desert looking for the valley that she fell in so she can tell the other women that were living in that dirty valley with the homemade rocking chairs. As she ran, she rejoiced, she twirled around in circles like a little girl. She stopped to dance. She sang a sweet melody. She felt so free! Yes, that's it. Free! That's the word. Free! She felt like dancing again. So she danced and danced and didn't care that she looked crazy dancing in the desert. Taliah was now free and she just had to tell somebody, anybody, everybody, especially those broken women in the valley. Where is that valley? I hope I don't get lost again trying to find it. I know I won't because God's spirit will lead the way. I am not worried. I will find the way because I have to go and tell the women in the valley about Jesus. Jesus! Oh what a powerful name she thought!! She said it again. Jesus! Oh, there is something about that name. Taliah continues to look for the valley. Good, there is the hole that I fell in that leads to the valley.

She climbed down the hole and went through tunnel looking for the women. They were in the corner sitting on the homemade rocking chairs talking. As Taliah was approaching them, they saw her and how different she looked; really different. They wondered what happened to her. She was glowing like a light or something. And she is smiling like she's really happy. I wonder why she has come back here. Did she forget something? Why would she come back here to this old valley?

"Hey, women of the valley, I have some good news! No, I have some great news. I met a man."

She met a man? What on earth is she talking about now? Then the old lady said, "Wait a minute. I thought you said you were through with men. And aren't you living with somebody now?"

"You don't understand. This is not a man but . . ."

"You said you met a man, now is he a man or not?"

"Well yeah, sort of. I mean . . . well . . . how can I say it? I'll just say it. He is the Messiah! The long awaited Messiah. The Messiah has come. And He has made me free. And you know what else He told me all about my life? He knew I had five husbands and that I was living with a man. Now how would He know that if He wasn't some sort of prophet or something?"

The skinny sick lady who believed in God and had kept the faith down through the years, said, "Are you sure. I mean is it really Him? I have been reading the good book and it said that the Messiah was coming. So do you think it's really Him? Are you sure? I mean, how do you know it's really Him?"

"I know it's Him. Something happened in my heart when I believed. It's Him, I tell you, it's Him! And guess what, I know He can heal you of your disease. He can make you well?"

"You think He can?"

"No, I know He can. Now come on, all of you, and get out of this valley. Everybody, come on, I want you all to meet him."

"Look Taliah, we have been down here in this valley for a long time and this is home for us. Plus there is no way out."

"Yes, there is a way out. Come on follow me. I will show you."

All the women seemed excited to follow Taliah except the old lady, Shamba. So she said, "Ya'll go on ahead; I am going to stay here. I am comfortable. I made these good comfortable old rocking chairs. I like my chairs and I done got used to this place. Now, ya'll go ahead without me. Just pray for me, ya here? Just pray for me."

Lori said, "No Shamba; you have to come. Come on. What she is talking about sounds good and real. This is just what we have been looking for. Years ago, we read in the Book of the Law that the Messiah would come. This may be Him. Can't you see she has changed? Look at her face. It's like she is glowing or something."

"Yeah, I see it, but I like the darkness, besides, where are we going to go, this here place I call is home. Go ahead. I'm too old and set in my ways, and I don't like change so I don't want to go on. Don't worry about me, I'll make it. Now go on."

"Are you sure?"

"Yes . . . I . . . I'm sure."

"Okay, but I don't think you are making a wise decision. You have to save your own soul, we can't do it for you. We really wish you would come."

"No go ahead . . . go on without me."

"Okay. Bye Shamba." All the ladies hugged Shamba and left with Taliah.

So with Taliah's help, the women managed to get out of the valley. They followed Taliah to the well and she was right. There He was. Jesus was at the well, watching and waiting for them to give Him their hearts. The men were still there with them. As they were approaching, the skinny lady asked Taliah, "Which one is He? Before Taliah could answer her, she made her way to Jesus and bowed down to kiss his feet. The women ran around Jesus asking him questions, laughing, touching his robe. The skinny woman joined Taliah and bowed down and kissed His feet.

Jesus asked her kindly, *"Do you want to get well."*

And she said, "Yes, yes I do Messiah."

Then Jesus asked her, *"Do you believe that I can heal you?"*

"Yes I believe." And instantly the woman was healed. She was overjoyed! She fell to His feet and worshipped Him, weeping uncontrollably. Jesus answered the other women kindly and spoke tenderly and gently to them. He was pleased they finally came to Him. They spoke with Him and they all believed and they too were all transformed. Then each woman went their own way, spreading the good news about Jesus. They eventually found another place to live, but at least it wasn't in that valley.

Taliah became an Evangelist and went back into her old town and saw her old husbands, family and friends that had abandoned her and all the people of the town. She felt no bitterness towards any of them because she had forgiven all that they had done to her. She even saw the men that raped her and told them about the Messiah. She became bold and confident and preached that the Messiah has come. He is here and has come to save you. The men of the town were curious and wanted to go see if what she said was true. They found Him and saw for themselves. They told her they didn't believe because of what she had told them, *(Obviously they still had some reservations of Taliah because of her past),* but because they had seen Him for themselves. Then, last but not least, she went home to tell her live in man, George, that she could not live in sin with him anymore. She was moving out.

Chapter Fifteen

Who Is This Man

Mark 4:41

"Who is this . . . that even the winds and the seas obey him?"

Taliah gets home and starts packing her bags. While she is packing, George comes around the corner. "Where have you been? I have been looking for you for the last few days. You didn't call me. Don't you know I was worried sick about you? I thought something had happened to you. Where were you?"

Taliah responds and says, "I told you I had to go to the well to get some water, but you just blew me off. You didn't listen. It's a long story, but I will tell you this - I am moving out. I'm leaving. I can't stay here anymore."

"What do you mean you are moving out?"

"George, listen. I met someone else. And you know what? He is the best thing that has ever happened to me?"

"What? You met someone else. Who is this man?"

"Who is this man? That's a very good question. I will tell you who He is." Taliah stops packing and looks at George with a big smile. "This Man is not a Man I tell you. He is God in flesh. He is the Son of God, yet, still a man. He is the Messiah and He has come to save us from our sins. He offered me this living water and I was a little hesitant at first. But there was something about the way He looked at me! Oh this Man has changed my life."

"Taliah what are you talking about? Are you insane? You have lost your mind. How could you do me like this?"

"You know what George, I don't even have time for this. And I really don't care what you think about me. I'm outta here. I gotta go tell everybody, anybody, somebody about Him. And, you should come and meet Him too."

"I'm not going anywhere. That man can't do anything for me."

"Oh yes He can. He can transform your life. He transformed mine. You know what . . . I really am wasting my time talking to you aren't I. I will pray for you and let God deal with you."

"Okay do that. I need much prayer."

"Okay, I will. Goodbye George."

Taliah starts walking towards the door with all of her things. "Wait . . . wait . . ." Taliah keeps walking. "Will you just wait a minute, please?"

"Okay George, what is it?"

"Look, I know that things haven't been right between us lately and I know it's my fault. I'm sorry. I really don't want you to go . . . cause I uh . . . I uh . . ."

"You what?"

"I love you. I really do. I don't know what I'm going to do without you. Please stay, I need you." He grabs her waist and pulls her close to him.

"No George. Stop. Look, I'm sorry, but I can't do this anymore. I have met Jesus and He is all I need right now. I can not remain in sin anymore."

"What, are you telling me you don't need me any more? You don't love me?" Taliah doesn't respond. "I asked you a question. Do you still love me?" Taliah looks at him seriously.

"Well, I uh . . . I do still love you . . . but . . ."

"Marry me then."

"What did you say?"

"I said . . ." He gets down on his knees and grabs her

hand. "Will you marry me?" Taliah is best friends with silence again. "Will you say something?"

"What do you want me to say?"

"Well, you can say yes."

"I don't know what to say, except . . . except . . ."

"Except what?"

"George, I'm sorry, but I can't. I can't marry you now. I know we talked about it before and I really wanted to get married again, and I couldn't wait to hear those words. But now everything has changed," she said with her facing lighting up. "See, I met someone else. And I have . . . I have fallen in love with him and I know He loves me. I love you, but this is a different kind of love. It's like it flows deep within my soul, to the core of my being, it makes me feel all bubbly inside. The way He looked at me with compassion. It was like his eyes were filled with love and piercing me straight through my heart.

It's not a human kind of love, George. It's a God kind of love. His Love made me whole instantly, just that quick. I really can't explain it. And you see, His Love is not just for me. It's for you too. It's for everyone that believes. He loves everyone; me, you, and the whole world!! Oh George, you have to meet him! I'm telling you, Jesus will change your life. He is what I've been searching for. As a matter of fact, He is what the whole world has been searching for. I have been searching for love in all the wrong faces and places. I have been searching for men to love me and all this time Jesus was who I really needed. After all these years, I didn't know that He was the one I have been looking for. Why was I so blind? How could I have . . ."

"Taliah, you know what? I have heard enough about this man named Jesus. You just met this man. How can you be in love with Him when you barely even know Him?"

"George, I don't think you heard a word I said. He is not an ordinary man. It is as though I have known him forever. I even felt in my spirit that before I was formed in my mother's womb, He knew me. Wow! And I'm sorry George, if you don't understand what I am saying, but again, I really have to go now. I'm sorry if I have hurt you but I can't live in sin anymore. I just can't. And you have to respect that."

"Okay, Taliah. I can't make you stay if you don't want to, and I can't make you marry me. But I think you are making a big mistake."

"Doing the right thing is not making a mistake. Us living together in sin and having sex was a mistake. Please forgive me. I wasn't in my right mind. Satan had my mind. But now I am thinking clearly and I am no longer entangled with the yoke of bondage. I am free now. I gave you my body then, but now, my body, my heart, and my soul, all belong to the Lord Jesus."

"Whatever, Taliah. You know . . . you ain't nothing but a . . ."

"You know what George, call me what you want, but I am not taking nothing from any man anymore, ever again. Never again will I be a victim of name calling. No more verbal abuse, no more physical abuse, no more rejection, no more nothing. I refuse to allow you or any man to talk to me that way. So again, I am outta here. And remember, you need to give your life to Christ. I will be praying that you will one day."

Taliah leaves with her bags in her hand, not looking back; although she knew George's ego was damaged, his pride had fallen to the floor, and his masculinity suddenly felt helpless with no strength. He knew there was nothing he could do. However, Taliah leaves and does not look back. Instead she leaves with a huge grin on her face. She was totally satisfied with what she just did and with no regrets. She didn't feel hurt. She didn't feel like a failure. She felt like she finally belonged to someone and that this someone adored her. She starts running and shouting and dancing and praising Jesus for making her whole and complete. No longer did she feel like she needed a man. At this point, all she wanted was Jesus. Her spirit was soaring so high now that she didn't want to come down, she did not want to cater to the desires of her flesh anymore. There was a time, before she met Jesus, that she would have reacted differently. But not this time. Now that she has met Jesus, her whole life has changed.

You may ask the question who is this man? This man is Jesus. He is the one that can set you free with His spirit, the living water. He died for you and He loves you unconditionally. He will give you His peace in the midst of confusion. He will give you His unconditional love when you feel you are unloved. He will give you His unspeakable joy even in sorrow. He will hold you in His arms when there is no one around to hold you. His spirit will comfort you in the times that you are down. When you are feeling lonely and need someone to hold you, His sweet presence will fill the air around you. His Word will feed you when you are hungry and is food for your soul. When you are thirsty, His water will quench your most desperate thirst. He will never leave you nor forsake you. He will be with you even until the end of the age. And He is waiting for you, lonely daughter, and divorced, single and married, broken woman. Come and drink of Him. Come now. He's waiting for you . . . at the well.

Chapter Sixteen

Healed, Set Free & Delivered

A Touch of Faith

Isaiah 53:6
"For I was wounded for your transgressions, bruised for your iniquities, the chastisement of your peace was upon me and by my stripes you are healed."

Taliah went back to the well to talk to Jesus and to spend some time with Him, but He was not there. She wondered where He went. She had to find Him. She wanted to spend some more time with him. She wanted to get to know Him. She enjoyed being with Him. Even if it was just for a few moments, she wanted more of Him. She needed more of Him. For all the years that she was with men, and looking to them to fulfill her needs and desires, never in a million years did she ever imagine that Jesus was who she had been looking for.

Jesus was what she needed. He was the one that could heal her broken heart, set her free and deliver her from bondage. Just that quick, all the wounds that were created by her past husbands and all the pain, all the hurt, all the abuse, all the rejection, was gone. Just like that, they were gone . . . instantly. He healed her just like that. She no longer felt any pain. Her heart was no longer broken. Jesus had mended her broken heart so that he could live there. No longer was she thirsty. Jesus quenched her thirst with his living water. How wonderful she must have felt to be whole and to know she was now whole?

Like Taliah, the woman who had the issue of blood for

twelve long years, in the book of Mark 5:22-34, was similar to Taliah, except her circumstance was physical. However, I'm sure being ill for twelve long years contributed to her spiritual deformity as well as an emotional imbalance. Can you imagine how this woman felt? Her spirit was broken; her emotions were out of whack. Well, wouldn't yours be? She had an issue of blood for twelve long years? I'm not sure what type of blood disease she had, however, some theologians suggest that what may have caused the flow of blood was a fibroid tumor on her uterus. But perhaps she was on her period for that length of time. Imagine that. Imagine losing blood frequently. She was probably weak and miserable, tired, hungry, crabby, and irritable. Just imagine if you were on your period for longer then seven days. This woman was losing blood for twelve long years. In addition to that, she had spent all of her money on physicians and no one could heal her. So there she was, broke and disgusted, sick, and in need of healing.

So when she heard about Jesus, she knew that He could heal her. One day Jesus was in town, and He was going around healing people. She wanted her healing too. Wouldn't you? So she made up her mind that if she could just touch His clothes she knew she would be made whole. She didn't guess, she didn't have any doubt, she had faith that if she could just touch Him, she knew she would be made whole.

The multitude that was thronging Jesus was surely blocking her way as there were several people following Him everywhere He went, even into houses. But she didn't care. She pressed her way through the crowds . . . on her hands and knees, which were probably sore from crawling on the dirty, rocky ground. Who cares about getting a few scars while you are on your way to a lifetime of freedom, healing and deliverance? Remember, in order to touch His hem she had to be on her knees. Per Levitical Law, she was considered to be unclean. She couldn't enter the temple because she was ceremonially unclean. She couldn't touch anybody. She had to say she was unclean. Oh how embarrassing that must have been for her going through the crowd of people! The people were probably whispering and mocking her wondering why she was out here? She shouldn't be out here. But she ignored them. She wasn't worried or concerned about what other people were saying about her, unlike Taliah in her miserable state, before she met Jesus. But this woman had to get to Jesus and nothing could stop her. She had to remain focused. *Note: don't pay any attention to what people say. Make up your mind, stay focused on your goal and keep your eyes on Jesus.*

So here it is, this woman with her issue. By the way, what is your issue, woman of God? Whatever it is, take it to the master. He can heal you. This woman knew if she could just touch his clothes, she would be made whole. She didn't guess, she didn't doubt. She demonstrated a touch of faith. She said she knew that she would be made whole, healed completely, instantly. Let me paint this picture for you. She makes her way through the crowd on her knees and finally she touches the hem of His garment and she was healed instantly. Her faith connected to Jesus and released the power that was within Him to heal her.

Did you get that? Her faith connected to the healing power that was within Him. She only touched His clothes, not Him. But because of her faith, it released the virtue and power of Him and unto her, healing her completely and instantly. Can you imagine how this woman felt after twelve long years of pain and suffering in her body? She was finally healed with just one touch! A touch of faith I can only imagine what was going on inside her. She stands up with excitement, joy, happiness, freedom, peace, love, strength. It's similar to the skinny woman in the valley who needed to be healed. She was healed instantly as well.

Jesus asked, *"Who touched me?"* Their reply was, "Master, the multitude is thronging you and pressing up against you and you ask who touched me?" Anyone could have touched you.

But Jesus says, *"No, this is not a normal touch. This touch was different. Somebody has touched me because virtue has left from me. I felt my power leave my body when this person touched me. This was a touch of faith."* So looking around Jesus asked, *"Who touched me?"* When the woman saw she was not hidden, she trembled, fell down at His feet, and said, "It was I, I touched you Lord." The Lord replied, *"Daughter be of good comfort. Thy faith has healed thee go in peace."*

So the woman leaves. She doesn't leave the same way she came, but she leaves healed, delivered and set free; rejoicing in her healing! Physically she was healed, but now spiritually, she has been set free, and emotionally, no longer was she depressed about her suffering. Imagine that! Healed, delivered and set free. She believed and had faith that if she would just touch Jesus, He would heal her.

See woman of God, you must have faith, believe and trust that Jesus will heal you. Now what is faith? I talked about this in a previous chapter. But *Faith is the substance of things hoped for and the evidence of things not seen.* Jesus said *if you have faith as small as a grain of a mustard seed you can say unto this mountain be thou removed and be cast into the sea and it shall be given unto you.* Now I don't think this necessarily means to go up to a mountain and say hey mountain get up and go jump in the sea. But I believe it means if you have faith, believe and trust God you can have whatever you say. But you must believe.

Of course, it must line up with the will and word of God as well. So if you need healing, believe that you are healed in Jesus name. At first Taliah didn't realize that she needed healing. Jesus had to show her that she needed it. Get it? At the well, He told her all about herself. He exposed all of her wounds from the past. And instantly, when she believed who He was, she was healed, delivered and set free. But she had to have faith in order to believe that she was healed. Like the woman with the issue of blood, she had to have faith to believe that she would be made whole. And that's exactly what happened. She came to Jesus one way, and after her faith touched Him, she left a different way. I can only imagine how this woman felt when she touched Him. Her whole life changed. So both of these women met Jesus and were healed, delivered and set free. How about you?

Chapter Seventeen

The Living Water
The Holy Spirit

John 16:7
"Nevertheless I tell you the truth; it is expedient for you that I go away: for if I go not away, the Comforter will not come unto you; but if I depart, I will send him unto you."

Women, this is one of the most powerful chapters in this book, because this chapter is dealing with the power of God residing within you, which is the Holy Spirit. If you are indeed a believer, a born again Christian, you should be empowered with the Holy Spirit to live a victorious life and to help you defeat the struggles that we have daily within our flesh. Some of you have been like Taliah. You have had five husbands. Well, maybe not quite five; maybe less or maybe more. Perhaps, live in boyfriends, ex-husbands, ex-fiances', baby daddies, etc. Whatever category they were in, you were left with a broken heart, misused, abused, mistreated, and rejected. You have been going from relationship to relationship searching for love in men and not allowing yourself time to heal. This is where I will share my testimony to help you.

In the past, I have had my share of men. I was abused physically, verbally and emotionally many, many years ago. I almost lost my life dealing with an ungodly man who was trying to strangle me to death. I was in a weakened and backslidden state during my younger years as a Christian before I was called into the ministry. And even though I was running from my calling and wasn't in my right mind, I was walking in the lusts of my flesh instead of walking and yielding to the spirit. I called on Jesus, and He rescued me, even in spite of my sins. Yes, even in the midst of my disobedience and my mess, and my so-called fun life while I was supposedly in church, and a pastor's daughter, partying with my friends and doing my things. He spared my life even when I forsook Him. I have always said, I left God, but God never left me. So when I called on the name *Jesus* in this abusive situation, the man stopped or should I say, the demonic spirit that was at work within him stopped strangling me, because I called on that name.

There is so much power and authority in that name. *For we wrestle not against flesh and blood, but against principalities, against powers against the rulers of the darkness of this world, against spiritual wickedness in high places.* We will deal with demonic forces in another chapter dealing with spiritual warfare. But it wasn't the man, per say, it was the demonic force of darkness within him and he was being controlled by that force. But when I used the name Jesus, I took the authority over that spirit that was trying to destroy my life. Praise God for sparing my life! I could have been dead.

Do you know how many women have been killed by the abuse from a boyfriend or husband? I praise God for protecting me. Even when I wasn't in my right mind and I too was searching for love in all the wrong faces. Not just faces but places. In the night clubs, partying and dancing, but inwardly feeling like I didn't belong there. I felt darkness all around me in those places. But I thank God for calling me back home. I thank my mother for her prayers because I know that it was her prayers that protected me while I was out there, endangering myself for a little pleasure.

I thank you, Jesus, for being there with me, even when I chose men over you. And twenty years later, after I took a drink of the living water, and after Jesus rescued me from myself, I am happily married to a wonderful man of God, (a Boaz) a family man who loves the Lord, loves his wife, loves his children, handsome, works hard, and takes care of his family. Hey! Wait a minute I feel like praising God for sending me one of his good boys, a Godly man who found his good thing . . . hold on . . . wait a minute . . . I feel a praise coming on . . . gotta get up and get my praise on . . . Okay I'm back. Now in addition to that, He released all the gifts in me to bring Him glory. I am now an ordained minister preaching and teaching the gospel wherever the Lord opens the doors. I am a women's conference speaker, a gospel play writer, a singer, a songwriter, a musician, and now an author. Hey! Wait a minute . . . I feel another praise dance coming on . . . excuse me for a minute while I go get my dance on . . . again.

Okay, I'm back. Forgive me. It's just that when I start thinking about all the gifts that God has given me, and all the blessings he has bestowed upon me, I can't help but to praise Him! And see, that's why I rejoice. That's why I worship. That's why I smile and that's why I dance. That's why I sing, that's why I write songs about Jesus, because no one or nothing can ever satisfy me like Jesus Christ of Nazareth can. My husband has it going on, but he is no comparison to Jesus Christ. God's Holy Spirit is real and He is filling me up everyday.

His Spirit is the living water, a wellspring running over up into everlasting life. It has indwelled me and lives inside of me. So whenever I need a drink, I can go inside of myself and drink. What does that mean to go inside of myself and drink? Well, if His Holy Spirit dwells within me and is alive, then I can drink of the living water springing up into everlasting life whenever I am thirsty. My well will never run dry. I can talk to Him anytime I want. I can ask Him for help when I am having problems. He will comfort me when I am down. He will bring all truth to my remembrance. Why? Because I asked Him to. *You do not have because you do not ask.*

Beloved, Jesus instructs you His Word to go to your prayer closet and pray in secret. He says, *when you pray, enter into your closet, and when you have shut the door, pray to thy Father which is in secret; and thy Father which sees in secret shall reward thee openly.* When I go to that secret place, His presence comes and surrounds me and He pours His love upon me. It's so much so that I wrote a song about it. It simply says;

I can't explain the way you make me feel.
When I am with you in that secret place
Where I find joy, so much joy.
And I know that you are real.,
Though I can't see, you are the one who sees me
And I can feel your presence all around me.
Nothing can compare to what I've found
Where would I be, where would I go
If your love did not capture me.
Now I'm lost inside your love, sent from above
It's not from this earth, it's heavenly
And it's given me so much peace . . .

And you will find His presence in that secret place. *In the presence of the Lord there is the fullness of joy;* So much joy unspeakable and full of His glory. He gives me a peace that surpasses all understanding. There is nothing like Him. I tell you absolutely nothing. I can't really even describe it! The world didn't give this and the world sho' can't take it away. Praise God! People get high on drugs, but why not get high on Jesus? Nothing can ever satisfy you like Jesus can. Alcohol, men, drugs, food, sex, shopping, money, girlfriends, boyfriends, family, friends or whatever you turn to, instead of God, (idols) these things or these people can never satisfy you like the spirit of God can.

If you don't have the Holy Spirit and you say you are a believer then you may need to check yourself. This may go against your theology and some of your traditional beliefs, religions and doctrines so fasten your seat belts. The reason why I am speaking so boldly and with confidence is because I have experienced Him and I have scriptures to support what I say. See, its one thing to say that you know something, but it's another thing to have experienced it and have evidence. Let me give you some scriptures. Romans 10:9 reads, *if you confess with your mouth and believe in thine heart that God raised Jesus from the dead, you shall be saved.* You first have to *believe* and when you believe the Holy Spirit comes to live within your heart. But then it reads you *shall* be saved.

What does that word *shall* mean? The Merriam Webster dictionary defines the word "shall" as to be able to express a command or exhortation, directives to express what is mandatory, used to express what is inevitable or *likely to happen in the future.* If you are indeed a believer and have accepted Jesus into your heart, then why not do everything Jesus says to do in His Word? There is more to do then just accepting Jesus into your heart. You need more of His Holy Spirit. You need the infilling of the Holy Spirit. *Have you received the Holy Ghost since you have believed?*

Paul asked the believers this same question. Let's go there because I really want to break this down for you, I will get back to Taliah in just a minute. But in Acts 19:2 and 6 says, *"Have ye received the Holy Ghost since ye believed? And they said unto him, we have not so much as heard whether there be any Holy Ghost"* (which a lot of Christians have heard about this but have yet experienced this spiritual encounter because of their traditional beliefs). *"And when Paul had laid his hands upon them, the Holy Ghost came on them; and they spake with tongues, and prophesied."* So, children of God, there is so much more for you when you believe. Yes! It's wonderful that you believe and have accepted Jesus into your heart, but there is so much more. We as Christians need power because of the struggles that we have in the flesh.

You may want to ask yourself if you've been born of the water and of the spirit. The baptism of water, through immersion, in Jesus' name is a representation of being buried with Christ. This represents that your old life died with Christ when you were buried in water and then resurrected because now you are starting a new life since you say that you believe? Jesus told His disciples in Matthew 28:19, *"Go ye therefore, and teach all nations, baptizing them in the name of the Father, and of the Son, and of the Holy Ghost."*

Note, Jesus himself told them to go and baptize them in the name of the father, the son and the Holy Ghost. Well, what is that name? Jesus. Jesus told his disciples to go and do this, and they did exactly what He told them to. People can take this scripture out of context, so let's go to Acts 8:14-16. *Now when the apostles which were at Jerusalem heard that Samaria had received the word of God, they sent unto them Peter and John, who when they were come down, prayed for them, and they received the Holy Ghost and the Holy Ghost fell on them and they were baptized in the name of the Lord Jesus.* However, despite of traditions, as long as we do all of what the Bible says, we can't go wrong.

The disciples baptized several in the name of Jesus Christ after John's baptism. Jesus also said in John 16:7, *"Nevertheless I tell you the truth, it is expedient for you that I go away: for if I go not away, the Comforter will not come unto you, but if I depart, I will send him unto you."* And then Jesus says, when He comes He will teach you all things. John 14:16 says, *"I will pray the Father, and He shall give you another comforter that he may abide with you forever, even the Spirit of truth; whom the world cannot receive, because it seeth him not, neither knoweth him: but ye know him; for he dwelleth with you, and shall be in you."* John 14:18, *"I will not leave you comfortless, I will come to you."* And John 14:26 says, *"And the Comforter, which is the Holy Ghost , whom the Father will send in my name, He shall teach you all things and bring all things to your remembrance, whatsoever I have said unto you. But when the comforter is come, whom I will send unto you from the father, yes, even the spirit of truth, which proceeds from the Father, He shall testify of me."* Later, Jesus told his disciples to wait for the promise. *And, being assembled together with them, commanded them that they should not depart from Jerusalem, but wait for the promise of the Father, which, saith he, ye have heard of me*. Once they believed, and was obedient and waited, the Holy Spirit came.

Acts 2:1-4 reads, *"And when the day of Pentecost was fully come, they were all with one accord in one place. And suddenly there came a sound from heaven as of a rushing mighty wind, and it filled all the house where they were sitting. And there appeared unto them cloven tongues like as of fire, and it sat upon each of them. And they were all filled with the Holy Ghost, and began to speak with other tongues, as the Spirit gave them utterance."* Now you have scripture references.

The Holy Spirit is real and is the living water. Jesus wants to abide with you forever. But he had to go so that the Comforter, or the *Paraclete* (the Greek word for Him), would come to abide inside of you, along side of you, on you, in you forever. In the Old Testament the Holy Spirit would come on a person but in the New Testament the Holy Spirit has come to live inside of you forever. Isn't that awesome? I don't know how I would have acted if I was there in the days of Jesus. Oh my, just to talk and walk with Him . . . just to see my Savior face to face. To see the miracles he performed would have been enough for me. I would have been like Mary at Jesus feet every day, unlike her sister Martha who was cumbered and worried about many things. I would have definitely been one of His followers and wouldn't care what people thought about me and I really don't now because I live my life for Jesus and Him alone. You shouldn't worry about what people say. Live your life for Jesus Christ. Don't be a people pleaser but become a God pleaser. Seek the approval of God, not man.

So believer of Jesus Christ and child of God, there is so much more to Christianity. If you believe, then you will do what He says for you to do in His Word. Yes you may believe in Jesus Christ but don't you want more of him? You need power. Don't you want power? It seems like everybody wants to tap into some kind of higher power. You have the magicians, astrologers, yoga meditations, spiritual rituals, satanic worship. People are looking for something to feed their spirit man. It seems when people start talking about these worldly things, it's acceptable and it's okay. But let a Christian start talking about the power of God, speaking in other tongues and different languages without having studied, then people think you are crazy and say things like, this is some kind of cult or something.

If you are a Christian, and you want the truth and you believe in the Bible, The Word of God, then you will believe in this wonderful gift that God has freely given you. The Holy Spirit is real and He is available to you as a gift. You need to be indwelled with power from on high. You need this power to defeat the enemy everyday, which is Satan. The gift of the Holy Spirit is for everyone who believes, and who open their hearts and mouths to receive Him. God will fill you. You need a continual filling of the Holy Spirit. It is a gift, it is free, and you do not have to work for it or pay for it. The price has already been paid by Jesus Christ. Right now if you do not have the power of the Holy Ghost, speaking in other tongues as the spirit of God gives utterance, pray and ask God for this wonderful gift. He can fill you now. Praise Him, thank Him for it and ask Him to fill you with His Holy Spirit with the evidence of speaking in other tongues, as the Spirit of God gives you utterance. Now I'm not talking about fake tongues that you are trying to do on your own. I'm talking about God pouring His spirit through you (as the spirit of God gives you utterance) causing you to speak in another language that only He can control, not you. You can't make it happen.

If it doesn't happen right away, then study the scriptures more and continue to pray, fast and ask for it. *As the spirit of God gives utterance.* What does that word "utterance" mean? It means an act of uttering, vocal expression, something uttered, a word or words uttered. So as you speak in tongues, you are not controlling it, but the Spirit of God utters and speaks Godly words through you which can only be understood if He gives you an interpretation. It's another language. You are speaking the wondrous works of God! And it feels so good! His warm presence hovers over you and it takes you to another place. Like people that smoke marijuana and do drugs to get high, why not get high on Jesus? Of course there is no comparison. The feeling is out of this world!

I will get back to Taliah in just a moment but please bear with me. I think it is important that you know about this and I want to give you as much information as possible. If this is your first time hearing about this, and perhaps your pastor doesn't teach speaking in tongues this all may sound crazy to you, but search the scriptures for yourself, and you will find that what I am saying is indeed true. It is in the Bible. The Holy Spirit is real. I have experienced it and so have many other Christians. Doesn't matter what religion you are, Presbyterian, Apostolic, Christian, Baptist, COGIC, Lutheran, you can be filled with the power of the Holy Spirit. So do me a favor, pray right now and ask that you be filled with His power if not now, soon. And if you have questions about it, ask your pastor first and also ask the Holy Spirit to lead you and guide you to the truth and He will teach you all things. Let's pray together my sister or brother;

> *Heavenly Father, we come to you in the name of Jesus giving you thanks and praise for what you have done for us. We thank you for granting us access through Jesus Christ, Therefore, we come boldly to the throne of grace making are request known. We thank you for the wonderful gift of the Holy Ghost. I want an understanding of this power. Then once I know the truth, I want to be filled and I will tell others about it.*
>
> *Please fill me with the precious gift of the Holy Ghost. I want the gift that you have so freely given to us. If you don't feel me this moment, please fill me in the days to come as I study more about your spirit in your Word.*

I love you and believe in you, in Jesus name I pray.

Amen.

His Holy Spirit is the living water and is what you need to live a victorious Christian life. Okay, now back to Taliah.

Taliah's life changed instantly as soon as she believed and accepted the living water that He offered to her. She left rejoicing and praising Jesus. So much so, that she couldn't wait to tell everybody about this Living Water. But there was more for her. Once she believed, she wanted more of Him. She wanted to do everything right according to His Word. Don't you?

Beloved, Jesus says to you right now . . . *come and drink of my living water, there is so much more of me. But is your heart open to receive more?*

Chapter Eighteen

No Longer Thirsty

John 4:28
"The woman then left her waterpot, and went her way into the city . . ."

So Taliah meets Jesus. When she finally drinks of His living water, she drops her water bucket. It sounds really simple, but think about all that Taliah went through to get to the well . . . to get the water that she thought she needed. Then she realized that she no longer needed the water that she thought she needed to quench her thirst, so she dropped her water bucket when Jesus told her, *I that speak to you am He.* When she heard his voice, she no longer needed the water from the well. Even though she was naturally thirsty, Jesus quenched her natural thirst with a spiritual thirst by giving her freely a drink of His living water.

I think the significance of her dropping the water bucket is so powerful. Stop right now and picture how Taliah may have looked after she believed. She was so in awe that she dropped her water bucket. Think about it. She was thirsty and she had been on this long journey. She was tired, hot, and needed some water. Can you imagine how she felt when she got to the well, but then, to see some man sitting there? Not just a man, but a Jew, and Jews have no dealings with the Samaritans. He wasn't supposed to be on this side of town. And he had the nerve to ask her, a Samaritan woman, for a drink of water. And she hadn't even got her water after walking that long, hot desert with holes in her shoes and blisters on her feet. So when she finally reaches the well to fill her bucket with water and then to take a drink, He says, give me to drink. So Taliah thought. No. I am not giving you a drink and besides, you are a Jew and you ask for a drink of water from me, a Samaritan woman? No. No. No. Leave me alone Mr. Get your own drink. Jesus says, *woman if you knew who it was that was asking you for a drink, he would have given you living water.* Taliah was probably like, "Yeah right."

But then skipping down a few verses Jesus says, *"You know the water that you came out here for? The water that you thought you needed. The water that you thought would quench your thirst? If you drink of this water you will thirst again."*

"Well of course," Taliah thought, "I will thirst again Lord, this water is cold and refreshing. It's good, and yes, I will want more. You are absolutely right." But the water that Jesus was speaking about was spiritual, not natural.

So Jesus responds, and I am paraphrasing here;

"If you drink of the water that I shall give you, you will never thirst again. But the water that I shall give you shall be in you as a well of water springing up in to everlasting life. My water is better then your water. As a matter a fact, it's sweet, it's good, it's tasty, it's a spring of water that will well up inside of you, running over and overflowing within you. It's also pure and holy, it's alive, it's breathing and it is everlasting.

No longer will you have a thirst for the kind of water that you came out here for. No longer will you turn to the things of this world to satisfy your thirst. No longer will you turn to men to quench your thirst. All this time, I watched you and waited for you to come to me.

But you kept choosing men over me. And that's

why I allowed them to keep breaking your heart, because until you realized that I was what you needed, you would just have to keep getting your heart broken.

So there I was, watching . . . waiting . . . watching while you tried everybody else. But I knew one day you would come to me, so I began to draw you. When you were on your journey, climbing up the mountain, in your valley experience . . . in your hurt . . . in your pain, I was drawing you. And now I have you. I have filled you with my spirit and quenched your thirst."

So Taliah looks for Jesus. She wants to find the man who changed her life forever. She needs to find the one who quenched her thirst. She thought, "If I ever find Him again, I will never let Him go. I will stay with Him, I will follow Him wherever He goes. When I met Him at the well, He made me feel as though I was the most important person in the world. I felt like He had known me forever." So Taliah begins searching for Jesus.

As she enters the next town, she asks them if anyone has seen Jesus.

"Have I seen who?" a lady replied.

"Jesus. Don't you know Him? You haven't heard about Him? You know He is the one that has healed me. He has this living water that . . ."

"Living who? What on earth are you talking about young lady?"

"He is the living water, I tell you. Come with me, we can find him together. I will show you. Do you know if anyone in this town has been healed?"

"Well yeah. There was a blind man that was healed and I think a man with a shriveled hand and . . ."

"Well then He's here."

"Yeah, He's here somewhere. Can't you feel His Presence? He's here, and I'm going to find Him."

"Well, if He's that's good, I want to find Him too. I need some of this living water too and I need a healing as well, so I hope you find Him. He sounds like a nice Man. When you find Him, please let me know, so I can meet Him too. Bring Him back my way. I can't go with you now, but I do want to meet him. Will you bring Him back to me?"

"Yes I will. I will try, once I find Him."

So Taliah continues searching for Him. Then she sees a bunch of men in a circle and spots Jesus sitting down teaching them. Taliah runs towards Him shouting, "Jesus . . . oh Jesus!" Jesus stops teaching and looks at her.

"What is she doing here, isn't she that Samaritan woman?" The men whispered amongst themselves. But Jesus says, *"She is a friend of mine. And she has just as much right to be here as you do. In the kingdom of God there is neither male nor female. Hello, Taliah, how are you?"*

"I am fabulous now that I have found you again." She falls to her knees and worships Him at His feet. "Oh Jesus, can I stay with you? I want to follow you wherever you go."

"Of course you can my daughter. But you need to tell everybody you see about me first. Go. Go tell them how I have quenched your thirst. Tell them how you are no longer thirsty and that I am what they have been looking for, especially my daughters; the daughters of mine who do not know me yet — even the ones who have never had a father in their life. And I know that some of them have been hurt and misused by their fathers, but I am their father now and I will always be there. I will never leave them nor forsake them. I want them to taste and see that I am good, blessed are they if they trust me. I want them to drink of this living water that I have provided so freely for them. It's a gift. My Holy Spirit is a gift. Tell my daughters that are depressed and lonely and would like husbands, that I am their husband. I am Ishi, their husband. I am the bride groom and they are my bride, the church. Tell them

to get married to me. Once they marry me, I will send them God-fearing men who will treat them the way they deserve to be treated. Do you hear my daughter? Tell them."

"Yes, my Lord, I hear your call. I hear your voice, like a sheep hears their shepherd's voice. I hear you. I will tell them Lord, I will tell them." Taliah leaves rejoicing . . . singing . . . running . . . dancing in the wind . . . laughing and playing like a little child who has just received a new toy. She leaves Him enjoying the beautiful flowers in the grass, and enjoying the breeze in the wind. She was lost in the love of Jesus. She was so satisfied and full of Jesus that she was about to explode! She must tell everybody about her new found love. The world must know about this love.

Chapter Nineteen

A True Love Relationship

Song of Solomon 6:3
 "I am my Beloved, and my beloved is mine . . ."

Nowadays people are searching for love in all the wrong faces or places. I am going to focus on women right now and then I will deal with the man later. Most women tend to want to be loved by a man. It's wonderful to be loved by your father, your siblings, family or friends, but it is nothing like having a man of your own to love you. So, what happens is that, since women yearn to be loved by a man, they begin searching for Mr. Wonderful. And unfortunately, it starts at a very young age.

Little girls yearn for love and affection from their fathers and brothers. They already know that their mothers and sisters love them, but they yearn to be loved and to feel loved by a male figure, so they begin searching for love in all the wrong places. It usually starts with young girls in middle school who want to be noticed and want attention from boys. Then in high school, she starts dating. Not one, not two, but as many as she can. All because she realizes that she likes going on dates and loves the attention and affection that she receives from these young boys. But after she gives her time, her affection, her loving, and sometimes her body to the boy she ends up with a broken heart, a baby, or worse . . . with a sexually transmitted disease. Now girls, Christian or not, should not be giving their bodies to any boy because their body is the temple of the Holy Ghost. Remember, there are always consequences to sin. It is God's perfect will for women to save themselves for their husbands.

I know we are living in the 21st century where sex seems to be everywhere. Not just now in the movies, videos and TV shows, it is evident on billboards and on commercials. I understand that it is hard for a lady to keep herself through high school and college and especially when they go to parties and night clubs where a lot of the bad boys hang out. Not just bad boys, but the good boys too. Yes even the Christian boys or should I say, supposed to be Christian boys, who are looking for girls to be intimate with. But anyhow these young girls have turned into young women wanting and yearning for their needs to be met and desires to be fulfilled. So they begin their search in all the wrong places — school, college, hang out places and the night clubs and now the internet sites, looking for love. They may not have received love or affection at home from their father, so they begin yearning for it and looking for it elsewhere, but only to get their little expectant hearts broken, only to get rejected over and over again, only to have high hopes and expectations for marriage let down.

They begin to dress provocatively and seductively showing their goods that should be hidden; trying and wanting to get attention from men. Keep in mind young women who are reading this book, if you are exposing your goods, can I make it plain and keep it real, your cleavage, your thighs, your belly button, wearing those shorty short shorts, mini skits, tight jeans and whatever you young girls are wearing now days which shows your flesh; dressing like that is not lady like, nor modest in the eyes of God. And you won't attract good, saved anointed young men of God dressing like that. Yeah, they may notice you and may even ask you out. But bringing you home to mom or asking for your hand in marriage isn't happening. So you need to dress modestly. Respect yourself and others will respect you. Again, I can't stress the importance of this to young teenage girls. When you dress provocatively, you will get attention from men, but the wrong men. They may give these young girls so much attention that they end up raping them and getting what they want. Some young girls are dating older men and the older men are using them as prostitutes. Some get pregnant and have baby after baby not learning from their mistake.

Some have abortion after abortion. Some end up getting abused, misused, mistreated and taken advantage of. Some end up on the street, on drugs, in a gang, in a girl school, in juvenile, and the lists goes on. All of this happens because they are looking for love in all the wrong places. They go through all of this because they're trying to find love in all the wrong places. They are trying to find *a true love relationship*. Only to get their hearts broken, only to get rejected over and over again, only to have high hopes and expectations for marriage. They want to live the Cinderella story, the fairy tale of Prince Charming coming to rescue them on a white horse. They daydream of this only because they are starving for true love after going from man to man, still unsatisfied and empty, like a river without water. It doesn't make much sense does it? Because the water that they really need and crave is the living water, which is the Holy Spirit to fill them up like a well springing up into everlasting life.

One may ask the question, "Why does the human race need love so badly?" Well what better person to ask than the creator? The Jehovah Elohim, the one who created the heavens and the earth and the entire human race. God, who's name is Jesus, created us with this yearning for love so deep inside so that we would eventually come to him for this love. Because God is love. He left that hole inside of the soul so that only he could fill it. That's why nothing else can ever satisfy us, totally. People have turned to so many things to fill that void, like alcohol, drugs, money, sex, relationships, careers, family and friends, trying so desperately to fill a void that only Jesus can fill. One may asked the question, *what is love? What is true genuine love?* Is love the nice feeling you get when you are holding your child for the first time and watching them grow? Is love when you meet the man of your dreams and he kisses you, creating butterflies that fly around inside your stomach looking for a resting place?

What is love? Well, the Merriam Webster dictionary describes love as; affection, attachment, devotedness, devotion, fondness, passion a feeling of strong or constant regard for and dedication to someone, appetite, favor, like, liking, partiality, preference, taste; craving, crush, desire, infatuation, longing, lust, yearning; ardor, eagerness, enthusiasm, fervor, zeal; esteem, regard, respect; adoration, idolatry, worship; allegiance, fealty, fidelity, loyalty to, cherish, prize, treasure, value, delight (in), dig, enjoy, fancy, groove (on), like, relish, revel (in); admire, esteem, regard, respect, revere, reverence, venerate; enshrine, memorialize; adore, dote (on), idolize, worship. There are so many words to describe love. Wow! I will describe the biblical love in just a moment.

But Taliah was searching for this kind of love in her five husbands. She went through an awful lot of men trying to find this love, only to get her poor, little, fragile heart broken over and over again. She said she was finished with men, but when she met her boyfriend George, she started living with him, it showed that she still needed to be loved by a man. She didn't want to be alone, and she was still starving for love; trying to numb the pain by developing a relationship with someone else. Taliah didn't allow herself time to heal just like a lot of other women. She went from relationship to relationship trying to find a man to fill the void that only God could fill. But after all of her hurt, all of her pain, all of the rejections, all of the abuse, the hot desert that God allured her to, she sensed in her spirit that something was missing. She needed more then men. She needed more then the hugs, the affection, the taking care of, the house to live in, her soul was still starving for something more. She really didn't know what. All she knew is that she was still thirsty after getting several drinks of the water that she thought she needed.

Finally Jesus began to draw her. There He was, watching and waiting to show her what a true love relationship looked like. He wanted to give her a kind of love that was out of this world; a love that would last forever. A supernatural, unconditional, everlasting, never leave you kind of love. Not the Eros kind of love; the way a man and a woman feel. Not a Felio kind of love, which is experienced through friendships. It's an agape love, which is God's love that goes deeper than the ocean. It's enough to heal every broken spirit, every shattered heart, wipe every tear, heal every wound and fill every void. This love is out of this world. When Taliah met Jesus at the well, she experienced this love when she believed and took a drink of the living water that Jesus offered her. No longer was she desperate for a man to love her. All she could think about was Jesus, so much so that she had to find him. She wanted to be around him. She wanted more of Him. She wanted to get to know Him. She needed and yearned for His presence. She needed to hear His words to comfort her. She needed Him to speak to her again. She needed Him to allure her again.

And so she went searching for Him and she found Him. Jesus was there. He didn't reject her, He welcomed her with open arms, in front of all the men who were talking about her and whispering about her. Speaking of men, men want love too, some just don't know how to express what they need from their women. But Jesus wanted a relationship with her just as bad as she wanted one with Him. The love that Jesus poured on her at the well was so overwhelming that she needed more of this kind of love. Do you realize how powerful God's love is? Most women, or men for that matter, don't even realize this. If they did, they would have found Jesus before they found any man or woman. You can have everything in this life. You can be rich, have the nice home, the beautiful children, the perfect job, a wonderful husband, a wonderful wife. But if you don't have love, you have nothing. I am talking about the agape love, the selfless love, the unconditional love, which is God. Let me give you the biblical definition of love.

I Corinthians 13:1-8 says; "Though I speak with the tongues of men and of angels, and have not love, I am become as sounding brass, or a tinkling cymbal. And though I have the gift of prophecy, and understand all mysteries, and all knowledge; and though I have all faith, so that I could remove mountains, and have not love, I am nothing. And though I bestow all my goods to feed the poor, and though I give my body to be burned, and have not love, it profiteth me nothing. Love suffereth long, and is kind; Love envieth not; Love vaunteth not itself, is not puffed up, Love doesn't behave itself unseemly, seeketh not her own, is not easily provoked, thinketh no evil, rejoiceth not in iniquity, but rejoiceth in the truth; Beareth all things, believeth all things, hopeth all things, endureth all things. Love never fails."

Ladies, this is the kind of love that you need. Jesus is waiting at the well for you to drink of the living water to give you this kind a love. Single women of God, get married to Jesus. If you are not a believer, I encourage you to go find him. He said *seek and you shall find*. Find He whom your soul loveth and longs for. Find your beloved, as it says in Song of Solomon 6:3, *I am my Beloved, and my beloved is mine.* Give your entire life to Jesus Christ. Let Him love you like no other man can love you.

What you need in your life right now is none other than Jesus Christ. When you find Him and give your life to Him, totally, He will give you whatever you need. I don't want you to think that I have been saying that you shouldn't desire or love a man, I'm just saying never ever put a man before Jesus Christ. He must always come first. He is the lover of your soul. You need Him so that you may be able to love another and receive love. How can you expect to love a man the way that God has ordained you too, when you don't love Jesus?

You need to first love Jesus with all of your heart, so

that His spirit can teach you how to love yourself. Once you really love yourself then you won't allow yourself to be in those bad, unhealthy relationships. Jesus will teach you how to love yourself so that you are able to love another. Allow his love to heal you and make you whole and complete so that you may be able to love another completely. Having a relationship with Jesus Christ is your true love relationship.

You will find that when you fall in love with Jesus and you have a close relationship with him, meaning, talking to him everyday, spending time with him, spending time in his Word, worshipping him with your life, loving and serving others, especially the unlovable, you really won't be too interested or should I say there won't be an urgency to have a relationship with a man, because you are so satisfied with Jesus. Of course when you get satisfied and content with Jesus, I believe with all my heart that God will send you someone that can love you the way that you deserve to be loved.

Jesus is your knight in shining armor. He is your Prince Charming . . . your rescuer . . . your healer . . . your deliverer . . . your mind regulator . . . your redeemer. And he is madly in love with you, His bride, sister, spouse, and friend. And He wants a personal relationship with you. Isn't that great? Imagine that. The God who created the world wants a relationship with you. He is concerned about every detail of your life. He even knows the number of hairs on your head. So trust him. Please don't allow yourself to keep getting in situations and circumstances that cause you to get your heart broken. First, you must find Jesus. Then He will bring a good godly man into your life. But *seek ye first the kingdom of God and his righteousness and all of these things shall be added to you.* What things? Everything that you need, including a true love relationship with a man, this will be added unto you, if it is God's will. *For God so loved the world that he gave his only begotten son, that whosoever believeth in him, should not perish but have everlasting life.*

Chapter Twenty

The Joy of The Lord Is Your Strength

Psalm 16:11
"In the presence of the Lord, there is a fullness of joy."

Taliah seemed very excited after she met Jesus at the well. She had so much joy. It wasn't a joy the world could give. It was a joy that filled her soul from heaven above. It was a joy that made her smile a real smile, not fake or broken. He made her laugh, rejoice, run, dance, weep, even in spite of her circumstances. And actually, she no longer had any circumstances. She felt so free. She was free from all the heartache and pain that was caused in her life; free from the cares and worries of this world. Taliah realized now where her joy came from. It didn't come from men, it came from Jesus. *In the presence of the Lord there is the fullness of joy.* She now understands what the scriptures mean when it says, *this is the day the Lord has made, let us always rejoice and be glad in it.* This is the Lord's day. He created it. Why be down and discouraged? Be glad. Be happy. Choose to be happy.

I was talking to my sister on the phone the other day, and she was saying how she has made a choice to be happy. She said no longer is she worried about anything. She will no longer be down and out. She will no longer hold unforgiveness or bitterness inside. As soon as she made up her mind and chose to be happy, something transpired in her spirit. Suddenly she felt like smiling and laughing. Something awakened in her

He's Waiting At The Well

that she really couldn't explain. Her spirit was leaping with joy. And because her spirit was leaping with joy, her flesh, that old sinful nature, had to line up with her spirit. She was no longer weak, but strong. Now she understood what it meant in the scripture when it said, *when I am weak, yet I am I strong*. For *the Joy of the Lord is her strength. She cast all her cares upon him because she knew he cared for her.* She forgave those who hurt her and released it to God totally. Instantly she felt nothing but freedom, joy, love and peace. So you my sister, please don't worry about anything anymore, make a choice to be happy.

Sometimes we as women worry about so much. We worry about what we are going to wear. We worry about our children, our bodies getting older, our hair falling out, our future, our husbands, our health, our finances, our ministry, our destiny, our love life. There are so many things that we worry about. If we don't worry, we worry that we are not worrying. We even worry that we should be doing something, when you should be resting. Doesn't make sense does it? I am reminded of the story about Martha and Mary. There was a big feast about to happen and Martha was in the kitchen preparing dinner.

While Martha was in the kitchen, cleaning, cooking, cutting, and just preparing food for the dinner guests, Mary, her sister, was at Jesus feet. So Martha started to get disturbed and frustrated because Mary wasn't helping her in the kitchen. So she told Jesus, "Jesus, tell Mary to come help me?" But Jesus reply was, *"Martha, Martha, you are cumbered (or worried) about many things, but what Mary has chosen is good, (which is at my feet), and it will not be taken from her."* So in other words I can just hear Jesus saying something like this, *"Martha relax and take it easy. What are you so worried about? You worry about so many things that are not necessary. Mary is at peace and resting and worshipping at my feet. She has found joy, peace and contentment at my feet. Yes, I'm glad you are cooking and wanting to serve but you are complaining while you are doing it. Don't cook and prepare the food if you are not rejoicing while doing the job. You should not murmur and complain. Do you realize Martha how I feel when my children murmur and complain? Remember how I felt when my chosen people, the children of Israel murmured and complained in the wilderness? It really bothers me when my people murmur and complain. Sssssh, be quiet. Don't talk so much.*

For a meek and a quiet spirit is pleasing to me. Don't allow yourself to worry so much. Please don't worry. Cast all of your cares upon me because I care for you. Every burden, every problem big or small, I can handle them all. Just give it to me and trust me to do the rest. I care that much about you. Yes, even the little things. I just want you at my feet. Because at my feet, you will find joy, you will find peace, you will find rest, you will find life. You ought to try it sometimes Martha, better yet ask Mary how she felt when she was at my feet. Ask her how she felt after she got up from being at my feet. I want you to have my joy, my strength, my love, and my peace. I want you to be happy and content in me and me alone. Stop worrying about things that do not matter. I want you to have joy. In the presence of the Lord there is a fullness of joy."

I wonder how Martha felt after Jesus' response. She probably felt embarrassed that she had even asked.

According to Merriam's Webster dictionary, joy is a feeling or the emotion evoked by well-being, success, or good fortune or by the prospect of possessing what one desires, a state of well-being and contentment, happiness. It is a source of great satisfaction and a state of happiness or felicity, a source or cause of delight. But I describe joy, and I am speaking of the joy that only God gives, as a feeling that overrides any other feeling. When you find Jesus, Jesus gives you this kind of joy. Sometimes when people of the world want to feel happy or even try to numb the pain, they take some kind of drug or alcohol to make them happy. To make them laugh, dance or sing. But this type of joy is not right and it is only temporary. The joy that I speak of is a supernatural joy of the Lord that enables you to overlook your current circumstance. When you should be sad, you have joy. When your flesh wants to cry out, yell, scream, be angry, or hit, instead you have joy.

When you have the joy of the Lord, you could care less about other people. You don't seek the approval of people, but the approval of God and become God pleasers and not people pleasers. This joy makes you laugh when you are sad. And you know sometimes we as saints of the most high God do not laugh enough. Do you know that laughter is like a medicine? It is good for the soul. When I met my husband, Charles, the one thing that I loved and noticed about him was his laughter. He seemed to be full of so much joy! He had an unusual joyful laugh that made you want to laugh, even if what he was laughing at wasn't funny. Charles loves to laugh, and laughter is good for the soul.

Christian shouldn't be mean, and those that are mean know they are mean. People don't like being around them because they are mean spirited. They should learn to laugh sometimes, and loosen up a little bit. Get your praise on. Get some joy. If you have Holy Ghost power dwelling within you, you should have joy. Joy is one of the fruits of the spirit. Sometimes I think about how good God is and I feel like Jeremiah and David. Like Jeremiah because it's just like fire shut up in my bones and makes me want to run; and then like David, because I feel like dancing. David danced and couldn't care less that he was a King. His wife got jealous of him dancing, but he didn't care, he kept on dancing for the Lord. I'm sure David felt that joy that I am speaking about. As it says in II Samuel 6:14, *"David danced before the Lord with all his might."*

You know, sometimes I wonder how believers can say they are saved and filled with the Holy Spirit of God, but just sit down and don't move in church. When the choir sings or the praise team is worshipping the Lord, and God's presence comes in that place, a joyful noise is made unto the Lord so you can't help but to praise Him. You should at least clap your hands, wave, nod your head, shed a tear or something! Sometimes I feel like dancing and running around the church because God is so good. I can feel his presence so strong. Not because of the way the music is playing, not because of the sound of the drums, not because the choir is jamming, it's because I have a relationship with Him and I know Him. So when I hear lyrics in a song of worship about him offering praise to God, if I hear music praising the Lord with an anointed sound, I can't help but to rejoice and praise the Lord. Psalm 66:1-2 reads, *". . . make a joyful noise all ye lands. Sing forth the honor of his name make his praise glorious."* Then Psalm 35:5 reads, *". . . my soul shall be joyful in the Lord, it shall rejoice in his salvation."*

Taliah experienced this joy at the well. Remember how she responded after she met Jesus? She ran, rejoiced, danced, laughed, and had tears of joy. She had just met somebody that gave her exactly what she has been looking for all her life. If you want to experience joy, come now child, get a taste of Jesus and you will experience and receive an everlasting joy. This joy does not compare to the world's joy. The world's joy is only temporary. The joy of the Lord is everlasting. And he gives you strength. There's nothing like the joy of the Lord. This feeling is better then sex, drugs, or alcohol.

This joy is not of this world and the world certainly didn't give it to you. So if the world didn't give it to you, then the world certainly can't take it away. Nothing can ever satisfy you like the joy of the Lord. Don't let anything or anyone ever steal your joy or your peace. Satan will try to steal your joy from you, but don't let him. Give no place to the devil. Keep on rejoicing in the Lord. When you are going through sufferings or a fiery trial, don't think something strange happened to you. *Count it all joy that you can most gladly rejoice in your infirmities so that the power of Christ can rest upon you.*

When you are suffering, worship, praise, rejoice and be glad for the joy of the Lord is your strength. Now that you have this joy, go and tell somebody. Please, don't keep this joy for yourself. You have to share it with the world. Go and tell somebody: a woman, a child, a girl, a boy, a daughter, a mother, a sister, a wife. Someone is hurting and needs to know that the joy of the Lord is their strength. A single woman is sad, lonely and depressed and she needs to know about this joy. An old lady in the nursing home is lonely and has no family or friends, please tell her about the joy of Jesus. Nehemiah 8:10 says, *"Go your way, eat the fat, and drink the sweet, and send portions unto them for whom nothing is prepared: for this day is holy unto our Lord: neither be ye sorry; for the joy of the LORD is your strength."* In the presence of the Lord there is a fullness of joy!

Chapter Twenty-One

The Call

Mark 16:15
". . . And He said unto them, Go ye into all the world and preach the gospel to every creature."

After Taliah met Jesus, she had to go and tell somebody. Taliah wasn't aware of this, but actually, Jesus had chosen her and called her. She was already predestined before the foundations of the world to become an evangelist. After she met Jesus, she felt an urgency to go and tell the other women and the people of the town. Remember, before she met Jesus, she was lost and wandering and unaware of her calling like a lot of other people.

If I could describe Taliah's characteristics prior to Jesus changing her life, she was insecure, needy, lonely, depressed, unsure of herself, and she had low self esteem. Her emotions were unstable. She was broken, bruised, wounded, dying inside, and her soul was thirsty. But when she met Jesus, she became bold, confident, secure, sure of herself, forgiving, happy, content, a servant, loving, caring and overflowing with His love and peace. A transformation took place. She was changed. She was no longer the old Taliah. She was a new creature in Jesus Christ. She was totally different.

When people say they are Christians and their life has changed, does their life demonstrate and prove that they have changed? You should see some type of difference in them, shouldn't you? If you don't, then you may want to double check to see if they really have been born again. Everybody that says they are Christians may not be because their lives don't show it. They are still living as the world lives and doing the same things they were doing before. You should lose the desires of the world and start craving desires for God. If you are a Christian, then shouldn't your life reflect the characteristics of Christ?

You ought to be bold for Jesus and tell others what has happened to you. You can't be ashamed of Him, like Peter. Remember Peter? Peter was with Him all that time and said, "Lord, I will die with you." Jesus told Peter, *"Before the crock crows, you will deny me three times."* And you know what? That is exactly what happened. Peter denied Him when three people asked him if he was with Jesus during the crucifixion. He said he didn't know Him. I still don't understand how Peter could quickly change after he walked with Him and talked with Him. After he saw the miracles He performed. Even after he had dinner with Him. But as soon as Jesus was taken away, Peter became ashamed of Him and acted as though he didn't know Jesus. How could you? How can you be ashamed of someone that loves you so much and proves it? You were just walking with Him and talking with Him. You saw the miracles that He performed. He just helped you fish. You just ate dinner with Him. How could you act like you don't know Him and say you don't know Him?

What Peter should have said was that he was with Him and he most definitely knew Him and the words that he say are true. He should have been bold and told them about how Jesus set him free, and that He could set them free. This was an opportunity for Peter to witness. If you were Peter, what would you have done? Would you have also been ashamed of Him?

If you are a believer of Jesus Christ, you should be a bold witness for Him and *be not ashamed of the gospel of Jesus Christ, for it is the power of God.* Taliah was eager to be a witness and to do what God had called her to do. She knew what she was called to do. She wasn't confused. It was quite evident. Go into the world and preach the gospel. Tell them, all of them, that the Messiah was here and He has come to give you salvation. He has come to save you and will change your life. He has whatever you need. You no longer have to be thirsty for this world's water. But you, yes even you, can come and get a drink of the living water. Come and drink of a sweet, living water that is a well springing up into everlasting life. Taliah didn't guess her call because she met Jesus. When she drank of the living water, suddenly her way was clear. She had wisdom and clarity; she could see clearly now; she was on the right road, and she had joy, peace, love, faith, gentleness, faithfulness, meekness and self control. She knew which way to go. No longer was she afraid, no longer did she run. *For God has not given you the spirit of fear, but of power and of love and of a sound mind.*

This is a good place to make a note. Those of you who are reading this book and have a call on your life, I hope you are not running from the calling that God has placed upon your life. You were handpicked and chosen before you were even born. God said, *"Before you were even formed in your mother's womb, I knew thee."* You were *"predestined before the foundations of the world."* God chose you out of all of your family members. He chose you. Get up and answer your call and do what God has called you to do. There is more to this walk with Christ then just going to church every Sunday and Wednesday night Bible Studies. It is time for you to get busy and do what God has called you to do. You have felt the tugging and pulling at your heart. God is calling you. You have a job to do. The Holy Spirit is indeed at work within you. Yield to the Spirit of God, don't grieve Him. Go and tell somebody about the good news. Go into all the world, into all the nations and preach the good news of Jesus Christ. Don't become a runner like some people-running from their calling. Don't run like Jonah. Every time I think about the story of Jonah, I just can't imagine what he was thinking. How in the world can you run from the Almighty

God? Don't you realize who you are running from? Don't you know that He is the omniscient God (which means that He is all knowing)? He knows and sees everything that you do. After God had called Jonah, Jonah decided to run from Him. Jonah 1:3 says, *"But Jonah rose up to flee unto Tarshish from the presence of the Lord, and went down to Joppa. There he found a ship going to Tarshish, so he paid the fare thereof and went down into it and to go with them, so that he can flee from the presence of the Lord."* I still can't quite comprehend why Jonah thought he could run and hide from God in a ship. You can't run or hide from God. It doesn't matter where you go. If you leave a church, if you move out of state, out of the country or overseas, He will come looking for you. He will find you because He is omniscient which means that He knows everything.

So while Jonah was on the ship on his way to Joppa, a terrible storm came. Beloved, please don't let a storm come to shake you up and to get you to answer your call. Sometimes the Lord will allow things to happen in your life to get you down on your knees to pray so you will answer His call. Jonah gets on this ship and the storm was terrible. So terrible that the men on the ship wondered what was going on. What has caused this evil storm?

Something must have caused this storm. So they asked Jonah, and Jonah told them the truth. That's a good thing; at least Jonah didn't lie. He wasn't in denial. He knew he was the cause of the storm. So he informed the men that he was running from God. He told them to throw him overboard and the storm would cease. They really didn't want to do it, so they prayed and cried unto the Lord and said, *"We beseech thee, let us not perish for this man's life, lay not upon us innocent blood, for thou, O Lord, has done as it pleases thee."* So the sailors threw him overboard, then suddenly there was a great calm. The storm had ceased. But when they had thrown Jonah overboard, low and behold there was a big fish, we call it a whale, waiting for Jonah. God had already prepared this fish to swallow Jonah.

This is what I would call a whale experience for Jonah, because he didn't answer His call. Why didn't the whale eat Jonah? That wasn't the plan of God. God's plan was to allow this whale experience to occur so that Jonah would obey and do what God called him to do. I wonder what whale experience the Lord has prepared for you to get you to answer your call? Think about it. Again, the big fish swallowed Jonah. Even though it did not harm him, I believe that God used this time, three days and three nights in the belly of this stinking fish, to teach Jonah a lesson and to get him to answer the call that He placed on his life. To give you a type of typology of this, just like Jonah was in the belly of the whale, Jesus was in the heart of the earth, but would rise again. However, that's another story.

Finally, Jonah humbled himself and submitted to God's request and answered the call, which was to deliver the people of Nineveh. Jonah originally didn't want to go to this city because it was terrible. However, God had another plan. He was going to save the entire city through Jonah. I believe that is what Jesus wants to do through us who have been called today. He wants us to deliver his people in various cities throughout the world. He wants you to tell them the good news: *Jesus Christ is the Way, the Truth and the Life.* And there is no need to wonder or worry about how you will do what He has called you to do. If He called you to preach, teach, sing, pastor, to the office of the prophets, call of helps, a call to service, a call to encourage or whatever it may be, He will equip you to do the job that He has called you to do. He will even send people and resources your way to get the job done. Jesus equipped Taliah to do what she was called to do.

She had the living water and that is all that she needed. After she met Jesus, she remembered the women that she had met in the valley and she had to go and tell them that the Messiah had come and that He would set them free and heal them from all of their issues. She wanted them to experience what she had. She wanted them to know that someone cared about them and that they did not have to stay in the valley to die. The Messiah has come to set them free. Not only did she tell them, but she also told the people of the town. Not just the people, but the men that had abused her, rejected her, and divorced her. She didn't care.

She was free from the pride, the hurt, the bitterness, and the unforgiveness and told them all about Jesus. That's the wonderful thing about Jesus. When you meet him, pride has to go, because *a man's pride will bring him low.* The hurt and the pain that was created from the past by others have to go because Jesus carried the pain and burdens at the cross. Also, He gives you the ability to forgive others so there is no bitterness inside anymore. He enables you to forgive even the one who left you with an unhealed wound. You know the one who broke your heart and left you for another woman, that man that abused you physically, mentally and verbally, the one that you can't stand to be around. The one you call your enemy. Please love your enemy because God will prepare a table before you right in the midst of your enemies. He tells us to pray for enemies and love them. Pray also for those who despitefully use you and abuse you. Some of you are holding a lot of bitterness and unforgiveness in your heart and Jesus is waiting to free you from that. But you must release it and forgive. Jesus said, *"How can I forgive you and you can't even forgive your brother?"*

One of his disciples asked him how many times he should forgive his brother; was it seven times seven? The Lord replied and said, *"No seventy times seven."* In other words, you have to forgive your brother seventy times seven every day. That is four-hundred and ninety times a day! Wow! You have to forgive your brother so you can be free. You need to be free so you can run and tell somebody about Jesus and how He has set you free and delivered you from all anger, bitterness and strife. You can be healed from your sickness and diseases when you forgive those who have hurt you. When you release that hurt and learn to forgive for real, I believe that your healing can take place. Some people have illnesses because they are still holding on to unforgiveness and bitterness. I dare you to forgive that person right now. Release him or her to God and be thou healed in Jesus name.

Like Taliah, you need to go out and tell somebody, everybody, any body about the Love of Jesus with boldness and confidence. Whether you are witnessing on the streets, the grocery store, your job, or to family and friends, you must tell somebody. You should be an epistle, a letter to be read by many. Don't you realize who you are and what the Lord has done for you? If you did, you would be sharing the good news with everyone you see. Do you realize that you are the only Christ that some people will ever get to see? Can you imagine how large our Sunday services would be today, if everyone would witness to at least three to five people a week? What causes Christians to not want to invite others to church? Are they embarrassed or ashamed? Again, *be not ashamed of the gospel of Jesus Christ for it is the power of God.* So go, my sister, my brother, answer your call and do what God has called you to do. Go, run, and tell somebody. Share your testimony. Shout, sing, tell the world about the Savior! Tell them about the living water that is waiting for them at the well. And while you are on your way on your journey, please do not allow your flesh to stop you from doing what God has called you to do, because it will try. That's why you have to *crucify the flesh.*

Chapter Twenty-Two

Crucify
The Flesh

Galatians 5:24
    "And they that are Christ's have crucified the flesh with the affections and lust . . ."

After Taliah's divorce was final, and after she had moved into her new place, she was so excited about starting her new life with Jesus. No more men or husbands to deal with. She felt now she can live her life free of heartache and pain. No more abuse, no more pain, no more rejection, no more heartache, no more disappointments, no more tears, no more arguments, no more trying to be something that she's not. No more depending on her husbands for her own happiness. She was now free of all of this. Taliah spent the next few weeks fixing up and decorating her place she now calls home. Daily she would pray, sing songs of worship and meditate on God's Word, for it was food for her soul. One night after fixing herself dinner and sitting down eating alone, she suddenly felt lonely. Even though she just thought how good it was to finally have peace and not deal with all the problems, she still felt lonely. She realized that she really didn't have anybody. No one was there to eat dinner with her, no one to talk to or laugh with, and no one to share with. She didn't have any family to visit her or to invite over because they didn't want to have anything to do with her because of her previous promiscuous life and bad reputation. She never listened to anything any of them had to say anyway. Her mother was ashamed of her and her father disowned her. She didn't know where her siblings were. So there she was, sitting at the dinner table . . . alone.

When she finished eating, she cleaned off the table, washed the dishes, and then sat down on her couch. Silence became her companion. Her mind began to wander again. She started reminiscing on her past. She thought about her past husbands when they were good to her. She thought about the beginning when there was love, affection, communication, and love-making, which eventually turned into sex. But at least she had access to it and anytime she wanted it she could get it. Oh, if she could be held by a man again! If she could just go out on a date, if she could just smell the masculinity of a man. Her flesh was craving to be touched by a man — any man, that is.

It had been months since she had been touched. Her flesh was in rage. She was beginning to wish she had a man again. She sat on the couch lonely and yearning and closed her eyes for a minute. Depression was trying to stick his ugly head out, but then all of a sudden she thought, wait a minute, I can't think like this. I have been changed. I am no longer that old Taliah. Flesh, what are you doing? She decided she would *beat her body and bring it into subjection.* She had Jesus now, and Jesus meant more to her than gratifying the cravings of her flesh. She didn't want a man right now; she only wanted Jesus. And she wanted to please Him wholeheartedly. So she thought, he sees and knows everything that I do.

Taliah got on her knees and prayed; *"Oh, Jesus, I pray right now, help me. Help me to control my flesh. Please take these desires and bad thoughts away. I know that as long as I am in the flesh, there will be a struggle. I don't have a man now and I know that. Maybe one day you will feel that I'm ready to start a relationship with a man again, which now I am so content that I don't think I even want another man. However, I can't ignore the struggle in my flesh. If you can just teach me how to conquer my flesh, I think I would do just fine by myself. But if you would like to send me someone, that would be okay. I guess. But this time Lord, please send me a good one. A Christian, God-fearing man who loves you Lord. But until then, you have to help me to control the flesh. Please help me, Holy Spirit, not to fall in sin. Keep me from evil Lord."* Then Taliah was comforted by the Holy Spirit and did not fall into sin. She fell asleep peacefully, resting in the arms of the Lord. His presence and love comforted her. He heard the desperate cry in her flesh and came to rescue her. He is the one that created her, and knew what she was going through.

Women, pay close attention to what Taliah did. She did not pick up the phone to call her ex to come over and fulfill her desire. She didn't watch a bad movie. She didn't do anything to satisfy the cravings in her flesh. She simply prayed and asked God for help. Beloved, that's exactly what you need to do. When you are going through seasons of loneliness and yearnings in your flesh, you must learn to *crucify the flesh*. But I want you to be made aware of something; as long as you are in this mortal body on this earth, and until you receive your heavenly body, you are going to have struggles in the flesh and in the mind.

It doesn't matter how anointed or holy you may think you are. You will indeed always struggle in the flesh. You may even struggle with certain addictions which could be sex to gratify your flesh. You may be addicted to nicotine and crave cigarettes to calm your nerves. You may have an addiction to alcohol to numb the pain, to drugs to temporarily make you happy, food to relax your emotions and crave your appetite, to pain pills, cold medicines or whatever else your addiction may be. You may even be addicted to gambling your money away. All of these things are forms of addictions and could be hard habits to break. One of the addictions that I feel is necessary to elaborate on is food. People are addicted to food and really think it's okay. Being addicted to food is no better then being addicted to the previous things I have just mentioned.

A particular food that is addictive is sweets. Once you start eating sweets, you can't stop. The more you eat, the more you want. You ever notice the times that you crave sweets? Usually I crave sweets when my emotions are raging at a certain times of month (if you know what I mean). You have to fight that sugar craving. Ask God to help you fight it and He will. He may refer you back to fruits and vegetables and herbs, which are healthier for you than eating all of those sweets and the processed foods and foods that are hard to digest. So if you have a problem with eating, and you want to stop, ask God to help you. But you also have to help yourself.

There are people who have addictions in the flesh. As it reads in Galatians 5:19-21, *"Now the works of the flesh are manifest, which are these; Adultery, (having sex with someone else besides your spouse) fornication, (having sex outside of marriage) uncleanness, (all types of filth) lasciviousness, Idolatry, witchcraft, hatred, variance, emulations, wrath, strife, seditions, heresies, envyings, murders, drunkenness, revellings."* All of these are lusts of the flesh according to the scriptures. As you read this, examine yourself and see which one of these apply to you. These could be strongholds. I believe a lot of us have strongholds that need to be broken. Do you ever wonder why you still struggle in a particular area over and over again and it seems as though you can't break free of it?

You are trying to live a good life in Christ, walking rightly before Him, but there is still this struggle in the flesh? Again, it is because a stronghold has taken hold of you and also perhaps a generational curse has been handed down to you from your mother or father or grandparents and so on. My suggestion for you to break this stronghold is to fast, pray, and speak God's word over it. I believe that the stronghold will then be broken. You can conquer the lusts of the flesh no matter what it is as long as you believe and discipline yourself and depend on God's Word and the Holy Spirit to help you. There is nothing, absolutely nothing, too hard for God. But you must come to Him.

There will always be a struggle in the flesh. Once you decide to give your life to Christ completely, your flesh does not want to cooperate. You may want to do the right thing, but somehow, flesh ends up taking over. You can't do the good things that you want to do because the flesh somehow intervenes. The spirit is willing, but the flesh is weak. As the apostle Paul says in Romans 7:15-25, *"For that which I do I allow not: for what I would, that do I not; but what I hate, that do. If then I do that which I would not, I consent unto the law that it is good. Now then it is no more I that do it, but sin that dwelleth in me. For I know that in me (that is, in my flesh,) dwelleth no good thing: for to will is present with me; but how to perform that which is good I find not. For the good that I would I do not: but the evil which I would not, that I do. Now if I do that I would not, it is no more I that do it, but sin that dwelleth in me. I find then a law, that, when I would do good, evil is present with me. For I delight in the law of God after the inward man. But I see another law in my members, warring against the law of my mind, and bringing me into captivity to the law of sin which is in my members. O wretched man that I am, who shall deliver me from the body of this death? I thank God through Jesus Christ our Lord."* Confusing isn't it? I believe what this passage of scriptures is saying is that even though there is a war going on within the flesh, you can win through Jesus Christ.

Taliah didn't know Jesus when she was going from relationship to relationship. She did not allow herself time to heal. It was hard for her to crucify her flesh, because she felt she had to have a man. But when she met Jesus, even though she still had the cravings in her flesh, she was able to control them through Jesus Christ. She didn't give in to the craving. She prayed and immediately God helped her with the struggle. It's simple. All you have to do when you feel your flesh getting out of control and wanting to sin is to pray and ask the Holy Spirit to help you. When I say pray, I mean some serious prayer.

Not popcorn prayers, but praying for at least an hour. If you want results you have to increase your prayer time.

Jesus said to his disciples in the Garden of Gethsemane, *"What?" You can't watch with me for one hour? The spirit is willing but the flesh is weak."* However, if you have the gift of Holy Ghost with the evidence of speaking in other tongues as the spirit of God gives you utterance, you can pray in tongues. Don't feel bad if you have never spoken in tongues before. Just start praying and meditating on God's Word and ask God for the gift. But once you have received it, I would encourage you as you pray to pray in tongues as well as the understanding.

When you do this, you get a supernatural power from God. It's kind of like a deposit from heaven and it gives you the ability to conquer the flesh. It doesn't matter what kind of struggle you are having in the flesh. Pray in tongues or as Paul says, *"Pray in the spirit (speaking in other tongues,) but pray with the understanding also."* Some of you don't believe in speaking in tongues, you think it's crazy. But it's real. God gave a gift of the heavenly language to those who are receptive of it. When you pray in tongues, you are praying to God. Also, you are declaring the works of God. In addition to tongues, worship Him and start thanking Him for what He has done for you. When you do this, you forget you even had a problem within your flesh. This will help you to *walk in the spirit and you won't fulfill the lust of the flesh.*

If you are thinking bad or negative thoughts, *cast down every imagination, and every high thing that exalteth itself against the knowledge of God, and bring every thought into captivity to the obedience of Christ. Hide the Word within your heart, and you will not sin against him.* Beloved, I know that this is a lot that I just threw at you, but this walk with Christ is not going to be easy, so you need power. Also, can you imagine the way your life used to be, before Jesus Christ entered? I can and there's no way I would ever go back to that lifestyle. Taliah definitely didn't.

Chapter Twenty-Three

Spiritual Warfare

Ephesians 6:12

"For we wrestle not against flesh and blood but against principalities, against powers, against the rulers of the darkness of this world, against spiritual wickedness in high places . . ."

As we all know, there is a war going on in the spiritual realm. When you make your mind up to do the right thing, you end up doing what you don't want to do. As I mentioned in a previous chapter, the apostle Paul said there is always a struggle in the flesh. When you would do good, evil is present. Even though we can't see the spiritual world, it is more real than the natural world, Because before the natural world existed, there was the spiritual world. God spoke the natural world into existence.

Do you think Job knew that God and Satan were having a conversation about him? Of course not. In Job 1:1-7, God and Satan are having a conversation about Job's life. *The sons of God came to present themselves before the Lord, and Satan came also amongst them.* Sons of God were angels. So God asked Satan, *"Whence comest thou?"* (What are you doing here?) Because, of course, there are angels of light and angels of darkness and they may have gathered altogether. Even though we can't see them, angels do exist in the spiritual realm. *You may be entertaining angels unaware.*

Satan replies to God, *"I'm going to and fro in the earth*

and walking up and down in it." In other words, he is roaming the earth and roaring as a lion, seeking whom he may devour. He is looking to kill, to steal and to destroy whoever he can find not clothed in the armor of God. And we will talk more about this towards the end of this chapter.

God said, *"Well have you considered my servant Job? There is none like him. He's perfect. He's an upright man, one that fears God and escheweth evil."*

Satan answered the Lord and said, *"Does Job fear God for nought? Or do you think Job fears you for nothing? Haven't you made a hedge about him, and about his house, and about all that he hath on every side? Thou hast blessed the work of his hands, and his substance is increased in the land. But if you put forth thine hand now, and touch all that he has, he will curse thee to thy face."* In other words, the only reason he serves you and fears you is because you have made him rich. And if you take that away, he will curse you to your face.

And the LORD said unto Satan, *"Behold, all that he hath is in thy power; only upon himself put not forth thine hand. So Satan went forth from the presence of the LORD."* So you see, God gave Satan permission to attack Job. Because the Lord is Sovereign, He knows every activity under the heaven and in the heavens. All power is in His hands, even the power of Satan. So anything that you are going through He knows about it. He has allowed Satan to attack you.

As a believer, you must know and be made aware that Satan is busy and he is out to destroy you. Satan, Lucifer, Beelzebub, the Prince of Darkness, the Red Dragon, whatever his name is, he is looking to kill, steal, and destroy you. He wants to destroy your life, steal your peace and joy and eventually kill you. He wants to sift you as wheat and throw his fiery darts at you, and that's why you can't give place to the devil. Did you know that when you get angry, and you say bad things that are not Christ-like, and you can't shut up, that your tongue is set on fire by hell? James 3:6 says, *"and the tongue is a fire, a world of iniquity, so is the tongue among our members, that defileth the whole body, and setteth on fire the course of nature, and it is set on fire of hell."* That's why you can give no place to the devil in any area - especially your mouth. We, as women, need to watch our mouths. Watch what you say, and let no corrupt communication come out of your mouth. Do not open a door for Satan to come in and start his attack. Have you noticed when you say something wrong out of anger, you just keep on talking and it seems like you can't shut up? I have been there. It's because you have given place for the devil. As the scripture says, *your tongue, that little member is set on fire by hell.* Have you ever said things you really didn't mean during your emotional outbursts of anger and later you felt bad about it? The reason why you were feeling bad is because the Holy Spirit was convicting you.

So the next time your emotions starts to rage, immediately ask the Holy Spirit to help you be quiet. As a daughter of the King, you should want to please your Father. *A meek and quiet spirit is pleasing to the Lord.* So watch out for Satan's traps because he will trap you in whatever area he can.

There is indeed a spiritual warfare going on. It goes on within your flesh and within your mind. Satan will prey on a specific weakness within your flesh: addictions, old, bad habits, ex-boyfriends, food, and all kinds of stuff that makes no sense, and stuff you thought you were over and done with. He will deposit negative thoughts in your mind from out of nowhere, and you may wonder why you're thinking about it. If you are thinking negative or bad thoughts, they were deposited by Satan. That's why you can't dwell on it. II Corinthians 10:5 reads, *"Cast down imaginations, and every high thing that exalteth itself against the knowledge of God, and bring into captivity every thought to the obedience of Christ."* So you have to cast that negative thought down and replace those thoughts. As it reads in Philippians 4:8, *"Whatsoever things are lovely, whatsoever things are pure, whatsoever things are of good report, if there be any virtue and if there be any praise, think on these things."* So think on good things not bad things.

Jesus said, *"He who keeps his mind on me, I will keep him in perfect peace."* So keep your mind stayed on Jesus in every circumstance so that Satan won't try to steal your mind. He loves to attack women during their emotional state. He may drop things in your mind like depression, suicidal thoughts, and other things to try to get your mind not to be focused on God. That's why you have to fill your mind with the Word of God. It is so important that you meditate on God's Word. In addition, you have to put on the right kind of clothes. You need to have on God's clothes, which is the whole armor of God, *read Ephesians 6:10-18 and study it.* You need the Word of God to fight the enemy when he attacks. I'm sorry to say this, but there are many believers who have been saved for many years and do not realize the power in the Word of God. God's word is living and it's breathing. It's alive. Hebrews 4:12 reads, *"For the Word of God is quick and powerful, and sharper than any two-edged sword, piercing even to the dividing asunder of soul and spirit, and of the joints and marrow and is a discerner of the thoughts and intents of the heart."*

When you speak that word while Satan is attacking you, he has to leave. That's why it is important to know the Word. *Hide the word of God within your heart so you will not sin against the Lord.* Don't just be *hearers of the Word,* but become *doers of the Word* as well as practitioners of the Word of God, practicing it in your everyday life. Listen to the Bible on CD. Read it, study it, and meditate on it day and night; hide God's Word in your heart so you won't sin against Him.

Beware of Satan's trap. Taliah wasn't aware that Satan was using her many men to distract her, steal her mind, body, soul, spirit, peace and her joy. In the story of Job, remember when Satan said that Job would curse God to his face? Well, I believe that Satan deposited that negative thought into his wife when she said, *"Do you still want to retain your integrity? You ought to curse God and die."* Satan was trying to use Job's wife to get him to curse God and die. He used Job's wife's mouth to say what he had deposited into her mind. Even though Job was suffering, he said, *"You sound like a foolish woman talking. What? Shall we receive good at the hand of God and shall we not receive evil?"* In other words, the Lord giveth and the Lord taketh away. Regardless, blessed be the name of the Lord. So even though Satan was trying to use his wife, Job realized this and still did not sin. Satan used men to distract Taliah from turning to God. But now that she has met Jesus, she was able to withstand any test that may have come her way. And so can you. Please don't give up during the spiritual warfare. Be strong and courageous and trust Jesus to see you through this. This battle is not yours, it belongs to the Lord. And in the end, you will win. *No weapon that is formed against you shall prosper.* You are now free because of the blood of Jesus Christ.

Chapter Twenty-Four

Freedom From Bondage

Galatians 5:1
 "Stand Therefore in the liberty wherewith Christ hath made us free, and be not entangled with the yoke of bondage."

Taliah was walking down the road and suddenly the women from the valley ran up to her and said, "Taliah, Taliah come on. Hurry."

"Hello and greetings to you, too. Good to see you."

"Taliah we're sorry, but you've got to come with us."

"What's wrong? Why do you all look so nervous?"

"They have taken away the Messiah. They . . . they have taken away our Lord."

"What! Who? When? They who?"

"The Romans. They have captured Him and they are going to crucify Him."

Taliah falls to her knees, "No. Oh God, please no. Not my Jesus, not my Savior! They can't. They just can't. I just found Him."

One of the women said, "They already did. They are taking Him to the hill of Golgatha. He was almost there when we left to come get you. We heard all the commotion in the crowd and wanted to see what was going on. When I saw it . . . I . . . I . . . couldn't believe it. They were beating Him and mocking Him. They put a crown of thorns on His head. Oh Taliah, He was so bloody. Blood was everywhere. I couldn't bear to see Him that way. How could they do this to our Savior, our Lord, our Messiah? Why did He let them do this to Him?"

"Come on, we have to go and try to stop them. Come on."

Taliah and the women ran through the road and into town looking for Jesus. They found Him hanging there on the cross. Taliah ran through the crowd leading the women as they followed her to get to Jesus. But the Romans wouldn't let them get through. "No!" Taliah said. "No! Let Him go! Please let Him go! Please, take him down from that cross!"

"Woman, shut up." The Roman said. "Your King or Messiah, whatever you call him, will die tonight."

"Oh no, please don't kill Him. Please."

"It's a little too late for that lady," the Romans said.

Taliah and the women walked away crying. They were all with Mary, the mother of Jesus, and the other women that had been following Jesus, the other Mary and Martha. They all held each other, cried and prayed to God to stop this horrible thing that was happening. They hugged each other and went their separate ways, crying. Of course, the mother of Jesus, Mary and her followers stayed there with Jesus the whole time. Taliah walked away and went home. Once home, for four days she prayed and cried. She fell down on the floor and lay prostrate praying, crying and asking God, "Why did You let this happen to Your Son. Why?"

God replied almost immediately. *"Taliah, He had to die to free you from the bondage of sin. For He is the Way, the Truth and the Life. I will resurrect Him and on the third day He shall rise. He will ascend back to heaven where He came from. But I will send you another Comforter, my Holy Spirit and He will teach you all things. My Holy Spirit is . . . the living water which you got a taste of at the well. Remember? There is so much of my living water that I want to give you. There is so much more. My Spirit is a gift. I will give it to all those who ask. I will fill you with more of My Spirit if you will just ask. You can drink of My living water as often as you like. Don't hesitate to come and drink of the living water . . . come my daughter, come. For I will never leave you nor forsake you. I will always be with you, even unto the end of the world. Even though you don't see Me, you can fill My presence all around you. I am omnipresent. My presence is everywhere, but only a few are aware of it. My glory has filled the earth. I will fill you with so much more of My Spirit so much so that it will be overflowing, springing up into everlasting life. You will never be thirsty again. Go, be a witness for Me, My daughter. For Christ has made you free. You are no longer entangled with the yoke of bondage."*

Taliah had to pinch herself again to make sure this was real. Was this the voice of God speaking to her again? Was this a dream? However, she knew in her spirit that this was indeed the voice of God speaking to her. She felt such an amazing peace when He spoke. She felt the glory of God and His presence all around her. She worshipped and cried herself to sleep resting in the presence and peace of the Lord.

When Jesus died, the veil of the temple was rent in twain, which enables us now to come boldly to the throne of grace. In the Levitical Law, only the high priest was allowed to enter the presence of the Lord in the holy place and to make atonement for the people's sins once a year. But when Jesus died, His blood was shed on Calvary and He was resurrected by the power of God on the third day and ascended back to heaven. Again, this enables us now as believers in him to come boldly to the throne of grace. We don't need a high priest because of Jesus blood. We can enter into the presence of God anytime of day, anytime of night, anywhere. God has granted us access through the blood of Jesus Christ. We are no longer entangled with the yoke of the bondage of sin. Jesus has freed us from sin. Therefore, there is no condemnation to those who are in Christ Jesus. We are now free! Free to live . . . free to love . . . free to laugh . . . free to enjoy life more abundantly. Jesus said, *I have come that you might have life and have it more abundantly.* You are free. So don't remain entangled with the yoke of bondage. *The yoke has been destroyed from off thy neck because of the anointing* of Jesus Christ on your life. You are now free. Yes, free indeed. Because of salvation, you are free and therefore you can never fall away.

This gift that God has given us is too awesome. *For it is impossible for those who have once been enlightened and tasted of the heavenly gift and were made partakers of the Holy Ghost, and have tasted of the good word of God, and the powers of the world to come. If they shall fall away, to renew them again to repentance.* So in other words, why will you fall back into bondage after you have been freed. Why do people backslide? Why do they turn away? Why do they want to go back to bondage? It reminds me of the children of Israel when God used Moses to deliver them from Egypt and from the bondage of slavery under Pharaoh.

They wanted to go back because they didn't have the food or shelter that they use to have. Even though God delivered them out of bondage, took care of them in the wilderness, performed miracles for them, they still wanted to go back. Why would anyone want to go back to bondage when you have been set free and delivered? That's like a man or a woman who has been freed from prison telling the guard they want to return. The guard would think that the man or woman was crazy. Why would you want to go back to prison? Why would you get back involved in your old lifestyle, your old bad habits, and your old addictions when Jesus has made you free from all of that? Off with the old man, and on with the new. You are a new creature in Jesus Christ.

II Corinthians 5:17 states, *"Therefore if any man be in Christ, he is a new creature, old things are passed away, behold all things are become new."* Why would Taliah want to go back to the bad situations she was in?

Beloved, you have been free so don't fall back into the bondage of Satan. Satan will try to use your weaknesses from the past to try to get you to fall back into bondage. As you stay in the Word of God and pray daily without ceasing, you will be able to spiritually discern and recognize Satan's traps when he tries to get you to fall. Give him no place. You have been freed through the blood of Jesus Christ. Free indeed!

Chapter Twenty-Five

Sweet Worship

Psalm 95:6, 96:9

   "O come, let us worship and bow down: let us kneel before the LORD our maker. O worship the LORD in the beauty of holiness: fear before him, all the earth."

   Holy, holy, holy is the Lord God almighty. Who was and is and who is to come. For thou art worthy to receive glory and honor and power all things were created by him and for thy pleasure they are and were created. These are the words that the four beasts and the elders said in Revelation as they were worshipping Him. Do you realize how much power there is in worship?

   When you worship and praise God, He inhabits the praises of his people. Inhabits means to live in, dwell in, occupy, make your home in, reside in, populate. God actually dwells in your praise. Think about that for a moment. The presence of the Almighty God lives in your worship. When you see people worship, some may begin to cry, some may speak in other tongues, some may sing in tongues, some may fall to their knees, or wave their hands because they are so full of the presence of the Lord, some may weep uncontrollably.

   Why is it so hard for people to worship? Well first let's define the true meaning of worship. Worship means adoration, love, revere, pray, respect or devotion. When you worship someone, you adore, admire, respect, praise, honor, and reverence them. You really want to please them. When you think about God and His awesome beauty, you can't help but to worship Him. Worship Him just because of who He is. The Creator of the universe . . . the only wise God and Jehovah . . . the Prince of Peace . . . the Everlasting Father . . . the Savior of the World . . . the Alpha and the Omega . . . the Beginning and the End . . . the First the Last, the lover of your soul . . . your Redeemer . . . your deliverer . . . your healer . . . your friend. Wow! Can you believe this? How can you help not to worship a God like this? Shall I go on? This page couldn't hold the many attributes of God. So I am compelled to worship him.

People may worship God in all kind of different ways. Some may weep uncontrollably, some may just shed one tear, some may jump up and down and run around the church, some may speak in tongues or even sing in tongues. Some may fall to their knees because they can't stand in His presence. Some may shout, some may dance, some may lay prostrate, some may just sit quietly and enjoy the peace and presence of God on them. However you choose, just worship Him.

I have noticed that different cultures worship God in many different ways. It really doesn't matter what style the church worships, just as long as they worship. For we all were created to worship and praise Him. If we don't praise Him, then the rocks will cry out. I believe all nature worships Him, the fish of the sea and birds of the air, the flowers, mountains and the ocean as well. All of God's creations worship Him in some form or fashion. The whole world should know that God created them and that He is so good. As the psalmist David said, *Oh taste and see that the Lord he is good, blessed is the man that trusts in him.* As good and as mighty as our God is, He wants to be your friend and He wants a love relationship with you. He wanted one with Taliah so much that he was waiting for her at the well in the hot desert. His disciples went and got food, but He did not. Instead He sat on a well, waiting. He was in a place that Jews never went because of the hatred and division amongst the Samaritans and the Jews. But there at the well, where He gave her the living water, He explained what true worship was.

He said, *"You do not know what you should worship. But the Father is seeking those who will worship Him in spirit and in truth."* To worship in spirit means that the spirit or the soul of man, as influenced by the Holy Spirit, must worship God and have communion with him. That's why the soul needs Spiritual affections, which is shown in fervent prayers, supplications, and thanksgivings. This is a form of worship with an upright heart, in which God delights and is glorified.

The truth is the Word of God. All of God's Words are true. Therefore, we must worship Him this way for this type of worship satisfies God. In church, you can worship and praise Him by saying Hallelujah, which is the highest praise. You can sing songs of heartfelt worship, you can dance like David and praise the Lord. You can run around the church. All of that is good and I believe your acts of worship pleases the Lord.

He inhabits lives or dwells in our praises. As we worship and praise Him, His presence dwells there. And when you worship out of purity, free from sin, condemnation and guilt, this is indeed true sweet worship. The anointing of the Lord oozes out of you and it is felt by others around you. However, I feel the best way to worship the Lord is through your lifestyle. You must have a lifestyle of worship. Not just at church, but on your job you should worship. You should represent Christ in the workplace. They should know that you are indeed a Christian by the life that you lead on your job. Are you in the clicks? Are you sitting at the gossiping table at work? No, you are set apart for the world to see Christ in you. You are a living epistle. In the grocery store, you should demonstrate kindness in the line and not curse out the clerk because she is moving slowly. You should let someone go in front of you if necessary. You should put the shopping cart back where it belongs. Worship in your home. Your home should be a place of comfort and cleanliness. If Jesus came knocking at your door right now, would you have anything to hide? Would you shove clothes under the bed, sweep the dust under the rug, and hide the sex tapes? Would you tell Johnny to sneak out the back door, change your TV program, or change your music station? What are you hiding? You can't hide anything from God. If Jesus came and stood right outside your door right now, would He hear you cursing at your kids or yelling at your spouse? Will He hear the wrong kind of music being played? Would your refrigerator be filled with alcohol bottles and beer? You should live a sin-free life, pure and holy, for this is true worship.

When you worship God in church and your lifestyle outside of church is right before the eyes of God, you can lead and bring others into worship. Sweet worship. Pure, divine worship. God's presence will enter that place because His spirit smells sweet true worshipping in spirit and in truth. Let your praise be like incense to His nostrils. Oh, if unbelievers only knew how it feels to experience the true presence of God through sweet worship! It is far better than what the world uses to get high. The world's high and a Jesus high is no comparison. People get high on drugs, cocaine and alcohol and they have tried everything else. Why not get high on Jesus? When you learn how to worship God, something supernatural takes place within your spirit. Your problems and your cares seem so far away because you can cast all of them upon the Lord because He cares for you.

Taliah realized this when she met Him at the well and drank of the living water. He filled the hole in her soul and quenched the thirst. When you need a drink of the living water, just worship Him and He will fill you with His presence. However, when you worship, don't think that you are doing God a favor. Of course, he loves to be worshipped, but again, if we don't worship, the rocks will cry out. When we worship, it benefits us. Our soul, our spirit, tells us that we are in need of a Savior. When we worship, deliverance and healing comes. The bondage is broken. You are free. Peace comes, joy comes. You no longer feel stressed or burdened down with life's problems. Try it. You will see that what I'm saying is true.

One may ask the question, how should one worship God? First, you have to recognize who you are worshipping. You are worshipping the Holy awesome God in His majesty, splendor and glory. And you are but dust in His presence, and your sin stinks in His nostrils. So first, ask God to forgive you of any sin that you may have and to cleanse you of all unrighteousness, sins of omission and commission. He said, *if you confess your faults he is faithful and just to forgive you of your sin.* And don't act like you don't have any sin. The Bible says that *all have sinned and have come short of the glory of God.* So ask God to forgive you of your sins before you worship. Then once you have been cleansed, enter your place of worship.

You may have to create a sanctuary in your home, your basement, your church, your car, your office or wherever you can. However, when you start worshipping Him, His presence comes to dwell. You feel overwhelmed. It is a beautiful feeling. That's why I can't sit down. I'm not being boastful, but I consider myself to be a true worshipper that worships Him in spirit and in truth. I know Jesus personally. He has brought me through so much. So I can't help but to worship Him . . . to weep . . . to lift up my hands . . . to sing in tongues . . . to worship in a melody created by the Holy Spirit . . . write songs of worship . . . shout for joy . . . run and dance like David. Wow, I'm getting excited thinking about how good God is! I feel like worshipping Him right now. Hold on a minute . . . I feel a praise coming on . . . gotta get my worship on . . . Okay I'm back. God is so good!!!

Beloved, are you a true worshipper? Come join me in true worship. You have no idea what you are missing. This goes beyond the human mind, it's spiritual. Come, give Him your true intimate sweet worship. *O come, let us worship and bow down: let us kneel before the LORD our Maker. O worship the LORD in the beauty of holiness: fear before Him, all the earth.*

Chapter Twenty-Six

Resting
In Him

Mark 6:3 - Hebrews 3:9
   "Come with me to a quiet place by yourself . . . and get some rest. Therefore remaineth a rest for the people of God . . ."

There are various spiritual seasons that we must go through as born again believers. I talked about the different seasons in chapter 1. I dealt with the natural seasons, as well as the spiritual seasons. There is also a season called rest. This is a season that is unfamiliar. It is a time when you think you should be doing something, and really you should not be doing anything but resting. You feel as though you should be busy doing more than what you are doing. If you are a single woman, you feel you should be constantly doing something. Whether it is going back to school to finish a degree, (which is good and I will encourage you to do that if you have the time, education is very important).

Or, if you are a married with kids, you have your husband who needs your help, your kids need your undivided attention, not to mention your eight to five job, the families laundry which can consist of six to eight loads of clothes a week, cooking dinner every day, house work, ministry, time with friends, and also going back to school in the only spare time that you have. And then you need time to study and prepare sermons for upcoming engagements, women conferences, etc. You seem to have so much to do but not enough time to do it.

If you are a woman in ministry, you may wonder why the doors of opportunity haven't opened yet for your ministry. Didn't He say, *knock and the doors shall be opened unto you?* Well, you've been knocking but nobody seems to be opening the door. Well, let me give you a hint. If you are waiting for somebody to open the door, it's never going to open. However, if you are waiting for God to open the door, He will indeed open it, but in His own timing, not yours. And when He opens the doors, no man can shut it. And when He shuts the door, no man can open it. If you try to open the doors yourself, you will have to try to keep them open. And that's not possible. In your heart, you know what God has promised you, yet you haven't seen it come to pass yet.

Even though the Bible says be anxious for nothing, you tend to be anxious trying to make things happen. If we can just learn to trust God, wait on God, and cast all of our cares and concerns on Him, because He cares for us, God will work everything out for us. And know that God is working behind the scenes on your behalf. He is preparing the way before you. When you are able to totally surrender everything to Him, not half of it, but everything, He gives you his perfect peace. That peace that surpasses all understanding. He said, *he who keeps his mind on Me I will keep him in perfect peace.* This means that you have to keep your mind stayed and focused on Him. When you do this, it enables you to enter into that rest.

I believe Taliah did that when she met Jesus at the well. When she met Jesus, her whole life changed. She had the living water. She was on her way to entering into His rest, although she had some growing to do since she was a new believer. And if you are a new Christian, don't expect to be real spiritual and deep overnight. It is going to take some time. You would need to study the Bible, be faithful to Bible Studies and Sunday morning services, change your environment, change your friends, pray and worship. If you do this, you are on your way to becoming a victorious Christian. Hebrews 4 says, *"And God did rest on the seventh day from all His works. And in this place again, If they shall enter into My rest. For if Jesus had given them rest, then would He not afterward have spoken of another day? Therefore remaineth a rest for the people of God. For he that is entered into His rest, he also hath ceased from his own works, as God did from His."*

Now to simplify this, there is a rest for the people of God to enter there into it. If God Himself, who is majestic in all His glory, rested from all of his works on the Sabbath day, don't you think we should rest? I believe sometimes God allows things to happen in our lives to make us rest if we are stubborn and not allowing a time of rest. We can get so busy with the cares of this world. I think we should pick a day of rest. I personally pick Sunday as a day with the Lord. This is a day dedicated to the Lord. I spend time with family, but I still rest.

I try to just relax and bask in the presence of the Lord. What a feeling! Some people don't really know what it means to rest. Well, let me define rest for you. Rest is to relax, take it easy, take a break, put your feet up, chill, not doing anything, but resting and relaxing. Take time out for yourself. Pamper yourself. Take a bubble bath, listen to some good worship music and just chill in the presence of God. I think people should take a vacation at least once or twice a year, whether it is a family vacation, a couples' vacation, or by yourself, it is much needed and you deserve it. God wants you to have a time of rest and a time to enjoy your family. However, the ultimate rest is in Him. God wants us to be totally in rest and content in Him.

I am compelled to say that some of you who have lost loved ones, those whom were close to you, and they were also born again believers, are now resting with Jesus in heaven. No longer are they in any pain, no longer are they suffering, no more doctor appointments, no more medications to take, they are now resting in Jesus. It doesn't matter what state we as children of God are in, we have learned to be content in whatever state. Like the Apostle Paul said in Philippians 4:11, *"For I have learned, in whatsoever state I am, therewith to be content. I know both how to be abased, and I know how to abound: every where and in all things I am instructed both to be full and to be hungry, both to abound and to suffer need. But I can do all things through Christ which strengtheneth me."*

It didn't matter to Paul what his circumstances were. He learned to be content in whatever state he was in. That word content means, happy, satisfied, pleased, comfortable, at ease. You can experience all of these when you are at a place of rest in Jesus Christ. He wants you to rest in Him and know that He is your source of strength, your source of peace. There is a song that is coming to mind right now called total praise. I'm not sure who it is by, but the words go like this:

Lord I will lift mine eyes to the hills, knowing my help is coming from you. Your peace you give me, in time of the storms. You are the source of my strength, You are the strength of my life. I lift my hands in total praise to you.

This song is so powerful and has so much meaning. God is our source, without Him we are nothing. It is in Him that we live, move, and have our being. He gives us His peace. He gives us the ability to enter into His rest. God has always declared man's rest to be in Him. His love is the only real true happiness of the soul which causes one to believe and have faith in His Word and His promises. Believing in Jesus Christ and His love for you is the only way of entering into this rest.

When Jesus comes back for His people, He will give us a rest from this world. No more pain, no more sorrow, no more tears, no more heartache. We will have so much for which to look forward! As God said, *therefore, remaineth a rest for the people of God. If they would just enter therein.* And then He says, *come with me to a quite place, alone, and get some rest.*

See, sometimes we have to be alone. And I believe the

Lord allows things to happen in our lives so that we can have some alone time with Him, especially if you haven't given Him His time for the day. However, most women don't like to be alone, but neither do men. Again, God said it is not good for man to be alone. Although Taliah became a Christian, she missed having a man around because she always had one. But she turned to Jesus and He took away her loneliness and controlled the desires in her flesh. So Jesus simply says to you my sister, *come with me to a quiet place* . . . this quiet place could be a walk in the park, a walk on the beach, sitting on a blanket in front of a lake, a stay at a safe cabin in the woods, going to a women's retreat, wherever you can find peace and quiet.

You need to get away from the loud noises, away from pressure, away from the stresses of life. I personally love the beauty of nature. I love the sound of the rushing white waves and the beautiful view of the ocean. There is so much tranquility, so much peace. I don't know about you, but I yearn for peace. I yearn to go somewhere and rest in the presence of God, and rest in time spent alone with Him. Sometimes God will allow times of separation from other people so you can spend time alone with Him so you may be refreshed by His presence. He says again to you, beloved, *Come with me to a quiet place and get some rest.*

Chapter Twenty-Seven

A Servant In The Kingdom of God

II Timothy 2:24-25
"And the servant of the Lord must not strive; but be gentle unto all men, apt to teach, patient, in meekness instructing those that oppose themselves."

Now that the season of rest has passed, it is now time to get busy in the kingdom of God. It is time to serve the Lord with all the gifts that He has given you to edify the body of Christ. We are all servants in the Kingdom of God. It doesn't matter what your titles are. Some ministers get so messed up with titles such as Evangelist, Elder, Deacon, Missionary, Deaconess, Eldress, Bishop, Apostle, etc. These are all just titles. I'm not knocking titles, as I am an ordained minister, an Evangelist, but we are all simply called servants and all here to serve as servants in the Kingdom of God.

We need to use the gifts God has given us. There is so much to be done in the kingdom of God. But only a few will sacrifice their time and service. *The harvest is plentiful, but the laborers are few.* We need to figure out what our gifts and talents are and use them for the glory of God and to advance His kingdom. We need to use these gifts and serve in the church, community, home, jobs, nursing homes, shelters, and prisons. Wherever you can help serve, you need to serve. You first need to learn how to serve others. Serve your spouse, serve your children, serve your relatives, serve your neighbors, and serve your church. Forget about trying to serve yourself or please yourself, but instead serve others. Even Jesus did not please Himself. He stated He didn't come to be served, but to serve. Again, we need to learn how to forget about trying to please ourselves and learn to serve and please others.

You can serve in the church by using your gifts and talents in the body of Christ. There are various gifts in the church and different members in one body. That body is none other then the body of Christ.

I believe that all the members of the body each have special and unique gifts and talents. Think about this: the foot works differently than the hand and the arm works differently than the leg. But they all need each other in order to operate. Just like the members of our own body need each other, each member of the body of Christ needs each other. Not just the organization, but the entire body of Christ, the living organism, needs each other. Read I Corinthians 12:12-26. It talks more about how each of the members of the body need each other. We must learn and practice to serve others and please others, for this is what Christianity is all about being like Christ.

What are the characteristics of a servant? There's an easy way to define it, by the fruits of the Spirit. The fruits of the spirit are love, joy, peace, faith, long-suffering, goodness, meekness and gentleness. A person that is a servant of the Lord demonstrates these characteristics with no problem. They are able to love others including the un-loveable, and their enemies. They are able to deal with and respect the boss or anyone else that may make them feel uncomfortable. The person who serves will experience an unspeakable joy while serving others, not having any expectations. They encounter perfect peace because God gives them peace while they are serving, even in the midst of chaos. God will give His servants His peace, because the servant's mind is kept on Jesus while serving. He is not serving them, but serving unto God. You develop faith while you are serving in ministry.

When you have faith while you are serving, you are waiting on God, trusting God and believing that God is going to reward you for your servitude. Of course, you do not serve to be rewarded, but because you simply enjoy serving your Master, Jesus Christ the Lord. Don't you realize that as you are serving others, you are serving Christ? That's why it should be easy to serve your spouse and please him without murmuring and complaining. Because when you serve your husband, you are serving Christ. I have learned, and this took some time, that as you serve and please others without having a motive or expectations, you actually enjoy it. You develop so much peace.

For instance, if you have a job that you really don't like and you feel as though you are there temporarily, yet you are content, you can look at is as though you are there to serve and help others. You can develop an attitude of gratitude. You may be at work and see if there is anything you can do to make your boss's or coworkers' job easier. This is when you know you have become a true servant. You forget about yourself and your own desires and needs, and meet the needs of others. I believe God is very pleased with you when you think this way and make sacrifices for Him. And ultimately, He will bless you as you are serving.

II Timothy 2:24-25 says, *". . . and the servant of the Lord must not strive; but be gentle unto all men, apt to teach, patient, in meekness instructing those that oppose themselves."* If you are a servant of the Lord, you must be gentle, kind, patient, and apt to teach others who don't know the way. You must be meek and humble. You must clothe yourself with humility, love and servitude. When you serve others, I believe that you are demonstrating the love of God. Loving others and loving God is one of the greatest commandments. When you serve and love, blessings will come out of nowhere. You may serve in a church or a ministry, and then out of the blue, you get a blessing from Heaven. When you are busy serving in a ministry, your community or wherever the need is, God will indeed bless you.

I believe that Taliah served when she went and told the women in the valley about Jesus. She didn't care about going back down that hole to get to the valley; she had to help those women and tell them about Jesus. She was not only a witness, but she was serving when she went to the town to tell others about Jesus. Taliah also served in a lot of other ways that weren't mentioned before, such as serving the poor, helping the widows, visiting and praying for those who were sick. Anything that Taliah found that would bring glory to God, she wanted to do. She enjoyed doing it. She even cleaned houses and mopped floors. This was one of her jobs. It didn't pay much, but she enjoyed doing it. She became a humble servant.

Chapter Twenty-Eight

A Man Who Finds A Wife Finds A Good Thing

For The Single Woman

Proverbs 18:22
> *"Whoso findeth a wife findeth a good thing, and obtaineth favour from the Lord."*

After Taliah drank from the well, she began to grow in the Lord everyday. She had her moments of loneliness, but through it all, she learned to trust in Jesus. She continued to meditate on His word day and night. She made sure to spend time with Him everyday. She prayed, sang songs of worship, and helped her neighbors. She got a job and worked faithfully within the community as well as within the ministry in her church. She did this for about three to five years.

She was so busy serving the Lord consistently that she didn't notice him. Notice who? She didn't notice a man of God, in the church, watching her, observing her, inquiring about her. But she didn't care. She was so into the Lord, and letting her life shine to please the Lord, that she didn't see anybody watching her or even noticing her. And that was unusual for Taliah, because back in the day, she could definitely pick up if a man was admiring or noticing her.

He watched her while she served the elderly, the children, the pastor and his wife. And when I say watched her, that doesn't mean he was lusting after her. He just admired her beauty as she worshipped the Lord through her serving and giving to others. He noticed that her praise was for real. He noticed the light or glow coming from the anointing on her face as she worshipped. He was attracted to her anointing. She seemed so happy, he thought. So content, so much at peace. Who was this woman? He noticed how much she loved the Lord. He noticed her faithfulness to the church because he had been watching her for the last three months now. He was a faithful and good man of God who knew the Word of God. However, he was single with a teenage son.

Adam came from a good family background. He was raised as a good Christian boy since high school. He was very handsome, intelligent, and well established. He had never been married because he was waiting for the right one to come along. However, doing his college days, he got weak and fell in sin by getting mixed up with a Jezebel woman that was trying to bring him down. (I'm sure you are familiar with the Jezebel spirit. Watch out men, she is around, even in the church). This woman ended up getting pregnant with his child on purpose. However, it was his fault too for allowing this sin to happen.

After this incident though, he confessed his sins and remained in the church which now he had been attending for years. There were several women that were attracted to him, but he showed no interest. He loved the Lord with his whole heart and he wasn't interested in being a player. However, he did want to settle down one day and have a family. However, he was very particular and selective about choosing a wife. She had to be a born again believer, saved and filled with the spirit of God and serving God and of course, attractive. She had to be whole and complete. This young man was busy serving in the church and was a servant to the Pastor. He loved his mother and three sisters. He was a good man. One day, three months before, he noticed a nice looking lady in the church worshipping the Lord. So one Sunday he asked his mother during offering, "Mom, who is that woman?"

"Who are you talking about son?"

"The woman over there worshipping the Lord."

"Oh. That is Sis. Taliah. I don't know much about her. She's kind of quiet, don't say or socialize much, but I know she loves the Lord and serves very well in the church. I don't know anything about her family background. She hugs a few of the children after Sunday school. I believe she may be a Sunday school teacher or something. Why are you asking?"

"Well, I uh . . . I uh . . ." Adam stuttered.

"You uh what?"

"There's something different about that woman. She stands out above the rest."

"Well, why don't you quit asking me questions about her and go find out who she is after church?"

"Well, maybe I will."

They continued through the worship service and after they dismissed, Adam's mother nudged at him when Taliah walked passed. "There she is, boy. Go on and say something to her." But before he could get a chance, she had gotten away.

"Did she even notice me looking at her? Mom, you think she noticed me?"

"How could she? You were way back in the corner of the church. Why didn't you say something to her?"

"I was going to, but she didn't even look my way? She's not interested."

"How can you say that, and you don't even know the girl? Well, you missed out this time, just wait until next Sunday. And you will have enough time to think about your approach, 'cause you know how you men are, saying the wrong things."

"Oh mom, what are you talking about? All men are not the same. Well, I will wait until next Sunday and just see what happens." Next Sunday comes and Taliah walks past Adam again, still not noticing him. He finally says, "Hello and praise the Lord, I'm brother Adam."

Taliah looks up with a bright smile and says, "Well hello, brother Adam."

Adam almost dropped his mouth. He thought to

himself, "This woman is even more beautiful than I thought! And her smile. Wow! Her smile lights up the room." He was freezing up and didn't know what else to say.

"Uh, my hand . . ." Taliah says.

"Huh, excuse me?"

"My hand," Taliah said, "It would be nice if I can have my hand back."

"Oh, I'm sorry. Forgive me, please don't take that the wrong way."

"Oh I'm not. I was just wondering when I would get my hand back."

He laughed and let her hand go. "Did you enjoy the service Sis . . . Sis.?"

"Sis. Taliah and Yes I did. The Pastor spoke a really good word. My spirit is so full and lifted."

"I agree, I am full off the word as well; it was definitely food for my soul."

"It sure was . . ."

"You know, I was wondering, Sis. Taliah . . ."

"I'm sorry to interrupt you, Bro . . . Bro . . ."

"Bro. Adam."

"Okay Bro. Adam. I really am in a hurry right now, but it was really nice meeting you. I have to go."

"But . . . Okay, I will see you later?"

"Alright then Bro. Adam; see you later and have a great evening. Goodbye."

"You do the same, Sis Taliah . . . Goodbye." Taliah walks away. Adam finds his mother who was mingling with the other older women. "Mom did you see me?"

"See you? See you doing what?"

"Well, never mind. I guess you didn't. I will tell you about it later." He runs out the church to see if he sees her walking away, and she's gone. All week long at work, at home, he can't seem to get Taliah out of his mind. One night before Adam goes to bed, he falls to his knees and prays to God. "God,

I don't know what's going on and why I keep thinking about this woman, in a good way though. I can't seem to get her out of my mind. I really would like to spend some time with her and get to know her. If you are sending this woman to me, please let me know. Please give me a peace about this. I don't even know her, but I feel I have known her forever. She is so beautiful and I know she loves you, Lord. It is so important to me that she has a relationship with you, and I believe she does. Seems like our spirits our connecting, or maybe it's just my imagination. Lord, I don't want to pursue this woman if she is not the one. So hear my prayer, oh Lord. In Jesus name, amen." Adam went to bed.

The next Sunday, Adam sees Taliah after church and boldly says, "Praise the Lord, Sis. Taliah. How are you this Sunday morning?"

"I'm very well Bro. Adam, thank you for asking."

"That's good. Sis. Taliah, can I ask you something?"

"OK, what is it?"

"Well I wanted to know . . . I wanted to know if you would be interested in going out to dinner with me next Sunday after church. Wherever you would like to go, I would be delighted to take you."

"Well, I uh . . ."

"Sis. Taliah, you don't have to answer me now. I can tell you love the Lord and you have a relationship with Him, so why don't you first pray about it and maybe if you give me your number . . ."

"Bro. Adam, I'm sorry. I am really not interested in a relationship right now. I am so content and happy in Jesus I don't want anything to hinder or ruin my walk with Him. You know what I mean?"

"Yes, I really do," Adam said. "I have had my share in relationships, trust me you really don't want to know. However, I would like to know all about you. Perhaps we can discuss it over dinner next Sunday."

"Well, we will just have to see. I'm not sure at this point. I will definitely pray about it and let you know."

"Okay. Uh . . . don't you attend Bible Study on Wednesday nights? I think I remember seeing you"

"Yes, I do."

"So maybe . . . you can let me know your answer then?"

"Okay, I guess I can do that."

"Okay then. Enjoy your evening and I look forward to seeing you again on Wednesday."

"Okay Bro. Adam."

Taliah walks home and looks forward to enjoying her day with the Lord. She feels so refreshed after Sunday morning service. She wondered how anyone could not feel His presence in God's house. God is so amazing. She just wants to bask in the presence of the Lord all day long. And that is what she does. Taliah goes to the park and enjoys the beauty of God's creations. She notices the yellow butterflies as they dance in the wind. She notices the wind whistling through the trees. She can hear the beauty of the melody the birds sing as they fly high in the blue sky. Looking up in the sky, she notices the blueness of the sky and the white clouds.

Oh this world is so beautiful! God created this world for us to enjoy. She picks out some pink carnations and puts one in her hair. She runs and laughs because she knows she is free. So much joy and peace has awakened inside. She has no worry, no care. She has cast all of her cares, concerns, worries, problems, guilt, and condemnation on the Lord, because He cares for her. When all the men in her past rejected her, He took her in and cared for her. He holds her in His strong arms and comforts her with His presence everywhere she goes because He is omnipresent, He is everywhere at the same place, at the same time. Wow! Amazing. Not only that, but His Spirit is living inside of her so she is never alone. He is always with her. He carried all of her burdens to the cross. She stopped and began to weep uncontrollably because she thought about how good Jesus has been to her over the past year. How He has made her whole and complete since all of the problems she went through.

She thought about the very first time she met Jesus at the well and He gave her a drink of the living water that is still springing up within her like a well. She remembered the time that she saw Him crucified, the time that she heard God's voice speaking to her about the resurrection, that He rose from the dead, the time that she saw Him ascend into heaven, the time that He breathed on her with the others and said, *receive ye the Holy Ghost.* The time when she was filled with His Holy Spirit speaking in other tongues as the spirit of God gave her evidence, which empowered her to defeat the enemy and conquer the flesh. The time when she was baptized in water in Jesus name, symbolizing that she was buried with Christ and now resurrected with Him, this gave her a new life. It was a wonderful life! She was so lost in love with Jesus.

Later, as hours passed by, she remembered Bro. Adam and thought, "Why would I want to be in another relationship? I am so satisfied with you Jesus." However, she kind of sensed in her spirit that maybe Adam was a gift from God. Could he be? God knows that when He created us it was not good for man to be alone. So He created a desire within us to want companionship, to want to enjoy this beautiful life with another human being. However, this person has to love Jesus. They have to have a relationship with Jesus. They have to be whole. So Taliah said, "I don't want to go through all the mess that God has healed me from. The abuse, the pain, the betrayal, and the rejection. I can't do it. I won't do it. I am so at peace now. No, I will not go out with him."

This is a good place to take a note single women. If you are content in Jesus and you are able to live life without a man, that's wonderful. By all means, stay single. As the apostle Paul said, *I wish you would remain single as I am, but if you can't, it's better to marry than to burn with passion.* So if you would like to get married and you desire a husband, as most women do, (it is very few that don't. If they don't, they are in denial of their needs and wants as a woman) ask God about it. Pray and He will give you the desires of your heart. But in His own timing not yours. It may take one year, two years or ten years, but wait on the Lord and trust Him. Use this time to get close to Jesus. Get married to Him. Now I must add this here: if you are married to Jesus, you can't commit adultery. I'm going to say this again. If you are married to Jesus, then you cannot commit adultery. You should not be fornicating with anyone, because your body is the temple of the Holy Ghost. You should not let any man tamper with your goods. Keep your body, which is a temple that God's Spirit now resides in, pure and holy.

Again, I think this is important. If you have any desire within you for a husband, then ask God to send him your way and let you know that he is the one. He said you have not because you ask not. But when you do ask, you ask amiss or with the wrong motives. In addition, please don't be in denial about your needs. A lot of strong, independent, career oriented, beautiful women miss their gift from God because they feel they do not need a husband or they have been wounded by men in the past. They have put all men in the same category. So they act as though they have everything they need, but deep down, they are still yearning for a husband. And it's okay. If you have a yearning and a burning desire for a husband, take it to the Lord and wait for God to send you His best. Don't settle for less because of loneliness. Wait for God's best. Let God send you one of His good boys. And don't worry. He will find you. You don't have to go out looking. You don't have to get a worldly man and try to make him change, because that ain't happening. You can't make him change. Only God can. As long as you *seek ye first the kingdom of God and his righteousness, then all of these things shall be added unto you.* Everything that you need, including a man . . . a good one.

Just make sure during your single life that you use this time to get busy and pray always. You should not have too much idle time because the devil comes as a roaring lion seeking whom he can devour. So pray and ask God to help you control your flesh. You need to practice self-control, which is one of the fruits of the spirit. If you have the spirit of God residing within you, He will help you in your weakness.

Taliah is at home now and she prays to the Lord saying, *"Dear Heavenly Father I come to You in the name of Jesus giving you thanks and praise for what you have done. I thank you for all that you have done for me thus far. Now father, before I make a decision about going out with this man, Bro. Adam, I need your approval, 'cause You know how vulnerable I can be around a man. I don't want to do anything without asking You first. I want my life to be pleasing in Your sight, and you know how it used to be. You know the problems that I used to have with men. So if you are sending this man my way, and he is a true man of God, one of your sons, please give me a peace about it, because right now, I am so content and happy in you. However, I will admit, there is still a desire within me to want a good husband, because I never really had one. So please give me a peace about the decision I make. I ask all of these things, in Jesus name I pray . . . Amen."*

Taliah was sitting in Bible study on Wednesday night. She was just getting comfortable when Bro. Adam walked in and sat in her row. He waved at her and she smiled and she waved back. After Bible Study, Adam approached Taliah and said, "Praise the Lord Sis. Taliah. Have you decided yet? Will I have the pleasure of taking you out to dinner this Sunday?"

"Praise the Lord, Bro. Adam. Are you having a good evening?"

"Yes I am. I really enjoyed studying the scriptures tonight. The Word of God is so rich and I feel I am growing stronger and stronger every time I read it."

"Me too. I believe that God has so much to tell us through His Word, however, everyone doesn't have a spiritual ear to hear."

"You are right Sis. Taliah. What I would like to know, my sister, is if you would like to go out to dinner Sunday."

Taliah felt a peace about this brother, especially now that she asked God about him first. And she had never done this before. Usually, because of her past desperation, she would be so desperate for a date that she didn't ask God about him. She just wanted a man. So Taliah answers him this time and says, "Yes, I would like that."

"Okay, then that's just marvelous. Where would you like to go?"

"It doesn't matter. I'm sure you will find a nice place."

"I definitely will. Do you mind giving me your number so I can call you to confirm everything."

"Okay." So Taliah gives him her number and says, "Now I just want to tell you, Bro. Adam, I am not looking for a serious relationship. Just a friendship. So if you have anything else in mind, think again."

"Oh no; I understand completely."

Sunday comes and after church, Adam takes her to dinner. They talk, they laugh, they pray, they converse about everything and anything. Taliah felt so comfortable talking to him. He was totally different from the rest of her men. He was definitely a good guy. She felt that peace that she had prayed about. It felt as though she had known him forever. Their spirits were connecting, but she wasn't ready to tell him about her past. She wondered if he would still be interested if she told him she was married five times. "Of course not," she thought, not realizing that this is a true man of God who could care less about her past. Still, she didn't tell him about her background until a month into the relationship.

They walked through the park and held hands. He held her tightly like a gentleman should. He was very respectful of her. He spoke to her. He listened to her. He seemed like he cared about her goals and her dreams. They talked a lot about Jesus and how He had changed both of their lives. Adam told Taliah that he had been in a few relationships before, but nothing really serious. In his past, he had dated a young woman in the church who turned out to be a Jezebel. During the time that he was with her, he had gotten weak and vulnerable and ended up sinning and doing things he regretted later. Of course, he repented of his behavior, asked God to forgive him and knew that God did forgive him. But because of that sin, he now has a teenage son named Bobby, who he gets every other weekend. They have great times together as father and son. He feels he has a wonderful son and is a good father and would love to have a true family one day. However, he admits that he still has a fear of commitment, a fear of marriage, a fear of expressing his true emotions, a fear of rejection, a fear of failure, and a fear of giving his heart to a woman that could one day break it.

This is a good place to make a note. *What Adam, as well as other men, and women for that matter, need to realize is that fear is not of God and comes from the evil one. God has not given us a spirit of fear, but of power, and of love and of a sound mind. Sometimes people allow fear to stop them from getting their blessings. However, Satan may try to use fear to stop the blessing from coming into fruition. So my brother and my sister, please don't allow fear to stand in the way of God's blessings. Okay, back to Adam.* So he stayed away from relationships, but did ask God to help him conquer this fear. The more he prayed and developed a stronger relationship with Jesus Christ, the more he had of an understanding of who he was. However, he knew that relationships weren't his area of expertise. His area of expertise was fixing things around the house. He never really knew how to love a woman, let alone how to be a husband. He just recently learned how to be a good father. He shared all of this with her and she was quite surprised. Out of all the men she'd been with, he was the first one that opened up and expressed himself in that way. Taliah thought he was a little risky to open up that deeply. However, she liked it. She found that to be a very attractive quality. As a matter of fact, she found everything about him to be attractive. This man was almost too good to be true. But then again, all good and perfect gifts come from God, and she did ask God about him first because she realized, as other women should, *that in all thy ways you should acknowledge God, and He shall direct thy path.* Even when choosing the right man.

So Adam continued talking and he said, "Taliah, I shared a lot with you about my past. However, Jesus has changed my life. He has changed my heart. No longer is my heart hard and stony. No longer am I afraid of loving a woman. I admit, I don't really know much about relationships. But, with Jesus' help, I know I can do all things through Jesus Christ who strengthens me and He will help me."

At the end of their date, they prayed together and they both felt so much peace about this new relationship. They continued to date, have fun, attend church together, and hang out with relatives. She met his son, Bobby, and hung out with them on the weekends that he had him. She absolutely adored Bobby. Finally one day, a year later, Adam proposed to her as they were walking hand in hand along the beach. Adam got on his knees and asked Taliah to marry him. She has been enjoying this time with him so much and she didn't want to stop seeing him, but marriage? "Not again," she thought, "been there, done that. And besides, I need to tell him the truth about me. After he finds out about my past, he probably wouldn't want to marry me," she thought. So she prayed in her spirit softly, "Dear God, please let him except my past. Give me the right words to say."

While Adam was waiting for an answer on his knees, Taliah said, "I'm sorry Adam, please get up, there are some things that I need to tell you."

"How about an answer to my question first, Taliah?"

"I really need to talk to you first, okay?"

"Okay, Taliah," taking her hand again and kissing it,

"I'm listening." Taliah told Adam about her past. She told him everything. About her five husbands, her live-in boyfriend, the abuse, the rape, the betrayal, everything. She thought that he would no longer be interested in her once he found out how many husbands she has had and her past reputation with men. But Adam, said, "I don't care about any of that Taliah. I am so sorry for all the pain you had to go through. But thank God that He protected you and healed. You are now whole in Jesus." He pulls her close by her waist, holds her and whispers in her ear, "Please marry me Taliah . . . marry me. No one will every treat you as good I am going to treat you. Those men didn't know what they were doing, so I am glad they let you go. 'Cause now, hopefully you will be mine, forever. I will take good care of you and love you the way you deserve to be loved. I will love you so hard. Please marry me Taliah."

With tears streaming down her face, and wrapping her arms around him, she says, "Yes, yes Adam I will marry you." They kiss gently and hold each other while watching the moon and listening to the sounds of nature. It was as though they both heard God's voice speaking through the wind in the trees, as though He were in agreement. And He was, because He was the one that joined them together.

So they get married and live a beautiful Christian life the way that God ordained it. They prayed together, worshipped together, went to church together, and studied the Bible together. Seven years later, Adam and Taliah were still happy and still serving the Lord. God blessed them abundantly. There was no struggle financially because Adam was a working man and believed in working hard to take care of his family. They had everything they needed because they both had a relationship with Jesus Christ and He supplied their every need.

Adam bought Taliah a beautiful house that she turned into a home. He took care of her and she took care of him, and the house, as well. She still had a job, but God gave her the strength she needed to maintain her household. Adam loved her the way that Christ loved the church. She honored, respected, reverenced and served him. However, there was something else that she desired that she did not have. A child. She was barren. Adam also wanted a child in addition to Bobby, his teenage son. He wanted a family, especially by the woman that he loved. So they both touched and agreed in prayer, that God would bless her and open her womb so that she would get pregnant.

Taliah told Adam that if God did it for Hannah in the Bible, He could do it for her. So they both had faith and believed in the healing power of God. They prayed and fasted for a child for about six months. And finally, the miracle happened. God opened her womb and Taliah got pregnant. God blessed them with a beautiful set of twins. A girl and a boy. They raised their children believing in Jesus Christ. They trained them up in the way that they should go, so that when they become older, they will not depart from their Biblical teaching or Jesus.

God blessed their family and they all were happy and content in Jesus, the way that it was supposed to be from the beginning. Of course, as with any good couple, they had disagreements. But because of their deep love for one another and their willingness to keep the communication line open, they were able to solve any problem that came their way. God helped them and gave them both their hearts' desires because they both trusted the Lord and made Him first in their lives. God said, *seek ye first the kingdom of God and His righteousness and all of these things shall be added unto you.* This includes everything that you need in this life. They made Jesus first in their life and He gave them everything they needed.

Beloved, God will give you what you need, but only if you seek Him first. Trust and believe that it will happen, and it will. Single woman, a good godly man will find you as you trust, serve and wait on the Lord. *Wait on the Lord I say . . . wait.* God will send him when the season comes. But it will be in His own timing, not yours. So wait and don't get in a hurry or settle for anybody because of loneliness. Wait for God's best.

Chapter Twenty-Nine

He's Waiting
At The Well

Isaiah 43:19-20
"Behold, I will do a new thing; now it shall spring forth;
shall ye not know it? I will even make a way in the wilderness, and
rivers in the desert . . . I give waters in the wilderness, and rivers
in the desert, to give drink to my people . . . my chosen ones. This
people have I formed for myself; they shall bring forth my praise."

Beloved, Jesus will make a way for you in the wilderness, in the valley or in the desert. Wherever you are, He will meet you. Yes, the Master will meet you right where you are. In your tears . . . in your loneliness . . . in your struggles . . . in your weariness . . . in your pain . . . wherever you have been turning to fill that void within you, He will fill you with his living water. He is the river right in the middle of the desert. He is the "way out of no way" in the wilderness. Can you imagine that? He is the bitter water that has turned sweet. He is the fresh water out of the rock.

No longer are you bound with chains. Instead, you have been set free. No longer do you need a man to survive. No longer do you have to feel as though you are alone because Jesus said he would never leave you nor forsake you. Jesus is waiting for you at the well. He is waiting to show you. He is waiting to heal you, deliver you, and set you free from any and everything that may be hindering your walk with Him. He wants you to enjoy the beauty of the ocean that He has created for you. He wants you to live a long healthy life. He wants to quench your thirst. He wants you to drop the water bucket. Let go of every man that has hurt you in the past. Forgive, let go, let loose, and let God. Place your burdens at the Master's feet. Bow down and worship Him. He is waiting for you to humble yourself and seek Him first, over and above everything. Yes, including all of the men in your past that have hurt you and left you for dead, left you scarred, or torn and broken. But now you can watch Jesus put all your pieces back together again. Fall in love with Jesus. So here is a note to all of the women that may have had some type of struggle with men. It wasn't by chance that you picked up this book. This message is for you.

To the single, married, divorced, or widowed women: Jesus is waiting at the well for you. If you were or still are like Taliah, and you have been involved in several hurtful relationships similar to hers, Jesus is waiting at the well to heal you, to impart his wisdom, to give you a drink of his living water. If you are married to an alcoholic, turn him over to Jesus. Pray, pray, pray. Do you know how much power you have in prayer? Prayer changes things. Not just things, but everything. God can change his appetite from alcohol to an appetite for Him. Set an example and live a holy life in front of Him. You will win him by your behavior.

However, if he gets violent and attacks you and your life is in jeopardy, you need to ask God for wisdom to help you to make the right decision in leaving. If you are married to an abuser, seek counseling as I personally don't think that God wants you to be in an abusive relationship that is going to kill you. Jesus didn't come to kill you but to give you life. Satan has come to kill, steal and destroy you. You need to follow your husband, but only as he follows Christ. If he is abusing you, and hitting you upside your head, he is not following Christ. You need to get away from him as quickly as possible. This is not the kind of relationship God wants you to be in, especially if it is life threatening. The abusive man has severe anger problems, perhaps unhealed wounds from childhood and needs to seek professional help. Women who are being abused by boyfriends or husbands, let me give you some tips: It is not going to stop unless he wants help. You can try to make him go to church, but if he goes, he will go for you, not for himself. You can't make him love you the way that you deserve to be loved, so let him go and leave him in the hands of the Lord. This type of man needs years of professional help and he needs to attend church and Bible Study regularly. He also needs to drink of the living water that Jesus wants to give him at the well.

If you were an abused woman that left your husband and you are trying to heal, Jesus is waiting for you at the well. I know that you feel like you are not going to make it. You have been abused not only physically, but mentally and emotionally as well. You are vulnerable, insecure and you probably have some low self-esteem issues. However, Jesus is waiting for you at the well, waiting to heal you, waiting to see you through, waiting for you to drink of the living water that He so freely wants to give to you.

To the woman that has been married to the adulterer, you have permission to leave according to the Word of God. God hates divorce, but if he has committed adultery with another woman, (or if a woman commits adultery), you have the right to divorce. However, if you love him enough to accept his mistake, if it is not ongoing, and he has repented before God, and asked for your forgiveness, your first choice should be to try to work it out. I encourage you to, but if you can't, then you do have the right to divorce according to Scripture. However, you still have to forgive him and learn to trust so that you won't hold any bitterness in your heart.

To the woman that is in a controlling, non-affectionate, single like marriage and perhaps married to a workaholic husband: you really have to trust God to work it out and pray daily - not popcorn prayers, but hours of prayer. Pray in the spirit and pray with understanding as well. Lay prostrate on the threshing floor, kneel, however you choose, but you must reverence God when you pray. Tell God all about your husband at the altar and God will either begin to change him or change you. In most cases, it's you. You will win him by your Christ-like behavior, even in spite of your own desires.

God wants you both to be one in flesh, so if you are separate in everything that you do, that is not the plan of God. He said when a man leaves his mother and father he is to cleave to his wife, which means to hold to something firmly as if by adhesion. Separation is not good in a marriage. It gives place for the devil to come in. If there is no affection, meaning some form of touch whether it be a hug, a kiss, holding hands, playing footsie under the covers, then you need to start letting him know what you need. Women need affection. I believe that's why in the Bible it says to *render the affection that is due unto her.* God knows women need this because He created us. However, if you do not receive affection, why don't you try giving it and perhaps it will be reciprocated? Sow love, sow affection and you will reap the harvest.

Men need affection as well. However, they may disguise it or are too macho to admit they need it. Pray that your husband will meet Jesus at the well, so that he too can take a drink of His living water. Pray that your husband will develop a relationship with Jesus Christ. Once he has been born of the water and the Spirit and has developed an intimate relationship with Jesus Christ, and knows Jesus for real, he will be able to render the affection that is due unto you and love you as Christ loved the Church and gave Himself for it. How beautiful it is to see two walking together in unity with Jesus according to His Word! In order for that to happen, you, too, must do your part. You must submit to your husband as the head of the household. You must reverence and honor him, love him, die to self, and learn to please him and make him happy. As women, we were actually created for the man.

To the woman that is living with a man. My sister, you

know better. You have been feeling guilty and condemned for a while because you are living in sin. You have been trying to get this man to marry you. Why would he? He is enjoying the pleasures of marriage. He gets what he wants so he doesn't need papers. You really need to run. The Bible says be not yoked with unbelievers. So you need to run far away from him and ask God for forgiveness for living rebelliously in sin all those years. God will forgive you. Once you repent, there is no need to feel guilty and condemned anymore, just do something about it. Move out. If he loves you, he will do the right thing and marry you. But unfortunately, in most cases, these live-in situations do not last and each person ends up marrying someone else. So you see, living with a man before marriage to test the waters does not work. There is healing for you, woman of God.

Last but not least, for the woman that is already married to a good man. Do not depend on that man for happiness. Depend on God. We are all imperfect human beings and our expectations of our mates shouldn't be so high. Learn to love one another by serving one another without expectations. Stop fussing and nagging so much, wife. Instead, get quiet and still before the Lord. A meek and a quiet spirit is pleasing to Him. Serve your husband as though you are serving God, and be happy. Choose to be happy, choose to love and choose to be free in Jesus. Let Jesus love you and make you whole. He is waiting for you at the well. Waiting and watching while you try everything and everybody else. I would like to paint a picture for you. Can you imagine Jesus in all of His splendid glory and majesty, sitting down by the well waiting for you to come to Him? He says;

Come unto me, all ye that labour and are heavy laden, and I will give you rest. I am meek and lowly in heart: and ye shall find rest unto your souls. Take My yoke upon you and learn of Me, for My yoke is easy and My burden is light. I am the one that you need, stop searching for love in all the wrong places, I am Love. I have so much love to pour on and in you so that you can pour unto others.

I will fill you with My Holy Spirit, the Living Water, the comforter, which will teach you all things and will bring back the words that I have spoken to you.

My Spirit is a gift I so freely give to you, and will give you power to overcome the enemy. Meditate on My word day and night. Become doers of My word and not just hearers only. If you continue in My word, you are My disciples indeed. I, Jesus, am waiting for you at the well with a strong hand and outstretched arms. My mercy endures forever. I will give you life and I will give it to you more abundantly. I am the Bread of Life, the bread of God which cometh down from heaven, and gives life unto the world.

I am the Bread of Life: he that comes to Me shall never hunger; and he that believeth on Me shall never thirst. All that the Father gives Me shall come to Me; and him that cometh to Me I will in no wise cast out. For I came down from heaven, not to do Mine own will, but the will of Him that sent me. And this is the Father's will which hath sent Me, that of all which He hath given Me I should lose nothing, but should raise it up again at the last day. And this is the will of Him that sent me, that every one that believeth on Me, may have everlasting life.

My daughter . . . my bride . . . my sister . . . my spouse, I am so in love with you and am waiting patiently at the well for you to come to Me. I have been watching and waiting while you tried everything and everybody else, yet you are still left unsatisfied. Don't you realize now, that I am the only one that can satisfy you totally? So come unto me and drink.

Scripture References

- Proverbs 22:6
- Genesis 3:16
- Jonah 1:3
- John 21:12
- Psalm 34:8
- II Corinthians 5:17
- Romans 8:35
- Hebrews 13:5
- Nehemiah 8:10
- I Timothy 3:16
- Proverbs 25:28
- II Corinthians 12:9
- Luke 8:24
- Proverbs 26:11
- Ecclesiastes 2:1-11
- I Kings 19:12
- John 8:32
- Psalm 51:10
- Hosea 2:14

- Matthew 6:33
- James 4:14
- Acts 17:28
- John 1:1
- John 5:7
- John 3:16
- Galatians 1:10
- II Thessalonians 3:11
- I Timothy 5:13
- Joshua 24:15
- Psalm 42:5
- Proverbs 10:19
- James 3:6
- I Peter 3:4
- I Corinthians 7:3
- Matthew 7:15
- I John 1:1
- Romans 6:1
- Galatians 5:16

~ *Colossians 3:2*

~ *John 14:6*

~ *Proverbs 16:21*

~ *II Timothy 1:7*

~ *Isaiah 30:21*

~ *Jeremiah 1:5*

~ *James 4:3*

~ *Matthew 6:6*

~ *Romans 6:4*

~ *John 10:27*

~ *Luke 10:40*

~ *Romans 1:16*

~ *Ephesians 4:27*

~ *I Corinthians 9:27*

~ *II Corinthians 10:5*

~ *Hebrews 13:2*

~ *I Peter 3:4*

~ *Psalm 119:11*

~ *Hebrews 6:4*

~ *James 5:16*

~ *Hebrews 4:9*

~ *Luke 10:2*

About The Author

Crystal Duncan-Hogue has been a Christian for thirty-one years. She is an ordained minister and preaches and teaches the gospel of Jesus Christ wherever the Lord opens the doors. She is an author, singer, actress, pianist, songwriter, playwright, drama production director and bible teacher. She has ministered at numerous women's conferences. Crystal loves the Word of God and believes that Jesus can change anyone's life if they would only believe in Him.

A sought-after playwright, her first production, "Ready or Not Here I Come" (previously named, "The Rapture" and "A Revelation is Coming Are You Ready?"), was performed in Indianapolis, Chicago, and Champaign and received rave reviews. Crystal is currently producing a gospel CD entitled "Stand Still," which will be released 2008. When writing, she is inspired by the Holy Spirit and she strongly believes her many gifts were given to win souls for Jesus Christ and build up the body of Christ.

Crystal is happily married to Charles Hogue, a high school principal, and together they are raising there three children, Clarissa, Andrew, and Kahlil.